TELL ME THE ANSWER

BOOK 2

by
Indira Mukherjee

bluebird books

bluebird books

An imprint of Sachdeva Publications
4598/12-B, Ansari Road,
Darya Ganj, New Delhi-110002
Ph. : 011-23277655, 011-23287586
E-mail: bookpalacepublishers@yahoo.com

First Published in India
by Sachdeva Publications
Copyright © 1997 Sachdeva Publications, India
This edition first published in Sept. 1997
Reprint: 2009

ISBN 81-7582-000-4

Illustrated by
Keshaw Art Studio
Layout Design by
Microtech Computer Delhi
Printed at
D.N. OFFSET PRINTERS
Price: Rs. ▮▮▮▮

Contents

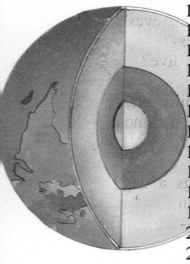

THE
WORLD
AROUND
US

HOW OTHER CREATURES LIVE?

HOW THINGS ARE MADE?

Are the seashells skeletons of sea creatures?

THE WORLD AROUND US

Why do volcanoes appear?

Did you know dew doesn't fall?

Neha said - "Ma'am, today at dawn I saw a lovely sight! In our garden, all the leaves held dewdrops in them. It seemed dew fell on them throughout the night."

Ma'am said - "I can imagine how lovely the sight must have been. But Neha, you will be surprised to know that dew does not fall at all! And dew, seen on the leaves of plants, is not all dew!

You must be thinking if dew doesn't fall, where does it come from? You all know that air holds moisture. And it's the warm air which holds much more water vapour than cold air. When the air comes in contact with a cool surface, some of that air becomes condensed and the moisture in it is deposited on the surface in tiny drops. And this is dew.

Neha, a small part of the moisture seen on the leaves is dew but most of it has really come from the plant itself. The plant supplies the leaves with water from the soil. And through the pores of the leaves, the moisture comes out. But of course some of them are dew drops. Dew forms on grasses and on plants which have become cool."

What is fog?

Linda asked - "Ma'am, what is the difference between fog and cloud?"

Ma'am replied - "Actually there is no basic difference between a fog and a cloud except that a cloud floats high in the atmosphere. We can even say that a fog is a cloud in contact with the ground. When a cloud is on the surface of the earth or sea, it is called "Fog". They are usually caused by a cold current of air from above, meeting the warmer surface of the land or water.

Moreover as the earth cools at night, the lower air gets cooler. Where this cooler air meets the moist warmer air just above, fog forms."

Linda asked - "Ma'am, why don't the drops in the fog fall as rain?

Ma'am replied -" These drops are not

big enough to fall as rain. You must have seen that the fogs often seem denser than clouds. This is because the droplets are smaller in fog. A large number of small drops absorb more light than a smaller number of larger drops as found in the clouds."

What causes smoke?

Shubho asked - "Ma'am, my mother says that Bangalore was a very healthy place till a few years back. But now it has also become smoky. What causes smoke?"

Ma'am replied - "Smoke is formed due to the incomplete burning of certain fuels. It means if the common fuels were burnt completely, there would be no smoke. What do the fuels have in them?

The fuels have carbon, oxygen, hydrogen, nitrogen, a little sulphur. If these fuels were burnt completely, the final product would be carbon dioxide, water vapour and free nitrogen. These all are harmless.

For complete burning, a fuel needs enough air for full oxidation at a high temperature. It's being said that these conditions are difficult to obtain especially with solid fuels and so the result is smoke." Shubho asked - "Ma'am, we all know that smoke is very harmful for all of us. In industrial cities, the people are inhaling the harmful smoke. Why can't something be done about it?"

Ma'am replied - "It's the responsibility of industries to do something about it. Many people are campaigning actively to cut down on smoke or to prevent it from doing damage. We should also join the campaign and try to find out ways to make a smoke free world."

What is smog?

Damini asked - "Ma'am, what is smog?" Ma'am replied - "We can say that smoky fog is what we call smog. When the combinations of different industrial gases get released into the air, it make up a kind of fog we call "smog". It makes people cough when they breath it. It can become poisonous.

You all know that dust is present in the air at all times. Dust may come from soil blowing, ocean spray, volcanic activity, forest fires, the exhaust from automobiles. Dust also come from industrial burning processes, what we see pouring out of the factory chimneys.

In big industrial cities, the amount of this type of dust is the greatest. It's causing health problems. People are campaigning against the industrial dust in the air. But the problem of dangerous dust in the air or "smog" still continues."

What is ozone?

Sanjeev asked - "Ma'am, it's being said that the industrial dust is destroying the Ozone layer. What is exactly Ozone?"

Ma'am replied - "Ozone is a form of oxygen. Ordinary oxygen molecules are made up of two oxygen atoms while ozone is made up of three oxygen atoms. In the upper atmosphere, it is formed by ultra-violet radiations. Ozone is also formed close to earth during lightening storms. X - ray and electrical equipments also form ozone. When metal is being cut with an Oxygen torch, blue sparks shoots off which means ozone is being formed."

Sanjeev asked - "Ma'am, what is the Ozone layer?"

Ma'am replied - "The earth is surrounded by a thick blanket of air - "the atmosphere". This atmosphere is divided into layers - The bottom layer which is about 16 kilometres high, is the troposphere. The second layer of air, from 16 kilometer to 48 kilometer, is the stratosphere. Between 19 kilometer to 35 kilometer is the "Ozone layer". This layer shields us from certain dangerous rays sent by the sun. This ozone layer should be protected by us."

Why are there different kinds of clouds?

Megha asked - "Ma'am, no two clouds are exactly alike. And they are always changing their shapes. Why is it so?"

Ma'am replied - "We have different types of clouds because cloud forms at different heights and temperatures and they are composed of different particles. The highest clouds which are called "noctilucent" clouds may be up as high as 30 to 50 miles. The mother of pearl clouds are 12 to 18 miles high. These are composed of

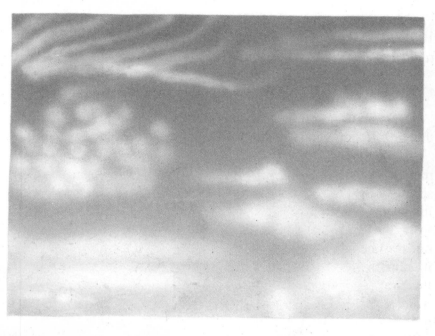

dust or water drops and they are seen only after sunset at night or before sunrise. Then there are clouds like "cirrus" which are five or more miles above the earth. They are feathery and threadlike and are made of tiny bits of ice.

Lower clouds are made of little drops of water. There are clouds which look like "cauliflower" and they bring thunder and storms.

The water vapour condenses into droplets to form clouds around many kinds of particles. There are dust particles blown from deserts, dry topsoil, volcanoes. There are tiny crystals of salt from the oceans, solid particles from the burning of coal and many other. These are the reasons why we have different kinds of clouds."

Where does it rain the most?

Disha said - "Ma'am, once we had gone to Cherrapunji and there it rained most of the time!"

Ma'am replied - "Cherrapunji is one of the places where it rains the most. The rainiest place in the world is Mount Waialeale, Hawaii, on the island of Kanai. It has an average yearly rainfall of 1,197 cms. Cherrapunji is the next rainiest place, with its yearly average of 1079 to 1143 cms. Once in a period of five days, 381 cms of rain fell on Cherrapunji! And in 1861, its rainfall added up to 2,300 cms!"

Disha asked - "Ma'am, how many droplets are there in a large raindrop?"

Ma'am replied - "It takes about 100,000,000 droplets to form one large raindrop! It would take about a million million droplets to make up a cloud one kilometer wide, one kilometer long and one kilometer deep. Such a cloud may have about 790 tonnes of water in droplet form and nearly 7,940 tonnes of water in water vapour form."

Where does a spring get water from?

Debabrata asked - "Ma'am, when we had gone to Nainital, I saw small springs on the hills from where water sprang out. Where does a spring get water from?

Ma'am replied - "A spring gets its water from the rains. When it rains, the rain water remains near the surface and some of it either evaporates

into the air or gets absorbed by the roots of the trees. The rest of the water soaks into the soil, goes as far down as the openings in the rocks will allow. Below the surface of the land, there is a zone where all the openings in the rocks are filled with water. This is called "the ground water zone". The upper surface of the water is called the "water table". We call it a "spring" when water finds a natural opening in the ground that is below the water table.

Some springs receive water from deep within the water zone throughout the year. And there are some springs which flow only in the rainy season when the water table is at its highest."

Which is the deepest ocean?

Rohan asked - "I saw the Indian Ocean when we went to Bombay. It's wonderful to live by the ocean, isn't it? Ma'am, which is the deepest ocean?"

Ma'am replied - "The ocean which has the greatest average depth is the Pacific Ocean. This is 4,281 metres. Next in average depth is the Indian Ocean which has an average of 3,963. The Atlantic is third with an average depth of 3,926 metres. The Baltic Sea is at the other extreme, with an average depth of only 55 metres.

The single deepest spot so far known is in the Pacific near Guam, with a depth of 10,790 metres. The next deepest spot is in the Atlantic off Puerto Rico where it measures 9,219. Hudson Bay, which is larger than many seas has its deepest point at only 183 metres."

Why is the ocean salty?

Anu asked - "Ma'am, why is the ocean salty? I mean how did so much salt get into the ocean?"

Ma'am replied - "Its really a mystery, we do know that salt gets dissolved in water and so it passes into the oceans with rain water. We all think that the salt of the earth's surface is constantly being dissolved and is passing into the ocean.

But does this explain the presence of such huge quantity of salt in the oceans?"

Anu asked - "How much is the quantity of salt in the oceans?"

Ma'am replied - "If all the oceans were dried up, so much salt would be left that a wall of salt could be built around the world - a wall 180 miles high and a mile thick! Enclosed seas, such as the Mediterranean and the Red sea, contain more salt in the water than the open seas. The Dead sea, which covers an area of about 340 square miles, contains about 10,523,000,000 tonnes of salt. On an average, a litre of sea water contains about 30 grams of salt. No wonder the ocean is salty."

What are the tidal waves?

Adil asked - "Ma'am, what are tidal waves?" Are they caused by winds or tides?"

Ma'am replied - "You will be surprised to know that tidal waves are caused neither by winds nor by tides. A tidal wave is caused by a disturbance on the bottom of the sea. Usually this is an earthquake that takes place on the ocean floor. Scientists have a special name for tidal waves. They call them by the Japanese name Tsunami. In 1896 seaquake of Japan (Kamaishi) waves went up to 30 metres hight."

Adil asked - "Ma'am, what happens when there are tidal waves?"

Ma'am replied - "In 1883, on August 27, the island of Krakatoa in the Dutch East Indies almost blew up. Due to the explosion, there were tidal waves which rose more than a hundred feet in the air. And these waves wiped out hundreds of villages. They speeded across the ocean at speed up to 700 miles an hour! And they were felt on the coasts of Australia and California, thousands of miles away!

In 1946 there was an earthquake on the ocean floor near the ALEUTIAN Islands. In less than five hours, the tidal waves travelled 2,000 miles and struck Hawaii. More than 170 people were drowned. Many houses and bridges were destroyed. Tidal waves are extremely destructive."

Which are the longest rivers in the world?

Rehana asked -"Ma'am, which are the longest rivers in the world?"

Ma'am replied - "The longest river needs the longest stretch of the land to flow through. This is the reason that in the continents of Asia, Africa, and America, we

find the longest rivers.

The longest river is the NILE - 6,670 kilometres long. Mississippi - Missouri is the second longest with its 6,420 kilometres. The upper Amazon follows it with 6,280 km. Next is the Yangtse - 5,800 km. the Ob-Irtysh in Russia is 5,410 km. the Rio de la plata, Argentina is 4,700 km. the Mekong is 4500 km and Russia's Volga is 3,530 km."

Rehana asked - "Ma'am, what about the European rivers?"

Ma'am replied - "The Danube, the longest river stretches to 2,860 km. The Rhine is 1,020 km. and the Loire is also 1,020 km."

Where are the highest waterfalls in the world?

Gurpreet asked - "Ma'am, Is not the Niagara falls the highest waterfalls in the world?"

Ma'am replied - "I am afraid, its not. The Niagara falls between Canada and USA is only 51 metres.

The world's highest waterfalls is in Venezuela. Water from the Carino river in Venezuela falls from the height of 972 metres at Angel's falls.

The second highest is Tugela in South Africa at 948 metres and the third is Yosemite with its 739 metres.

Utigard in Norway with 610 metres and the Sutherland falls in New Zealand, with 579 metres comes next.

But it's not the height which makes falls famous. We all have heard of the Niagara falls, which is only 51 metres and the African Victorial falls which is only 122 metres. When more people visit a particular spot, it becomes famous."

Which is the highest mountain in the world?

Akash asked - "Ma'am, which is the highest mountain in the world? Isn't it the Mount Everest?"

Ma'am replied - "That's right. The highest mountain above ground is Mount Everest. It is 8,848 metres high. The second highest is K2 or Mount Godwin Austen in Kashmir. It is 8,611 metres high. The highest mountain in North America is

Mckinley, which is 6,194 metres high. In Europe the highest is Mount Elbrus in Russia. It is 5,633 metres high. Kilimanjaro with 5,963 metres is the highest in Africa. In South America, the highest is Aconcagua on the Argentine - Chile border with its 6,969 metres height. In Australia, the highest mountain is Kosciusko which is 2,226 metres high.

All these mountains are above ground. Mauna Kea on the island of Hawaii is 4,205 metres above sea level and 4,877 metres below the sea. Its total height is 9,100 metres. It is not considered the highest because half of it is below the sea."

Why is it cooler on top of a mountain?

Natasha asked - "Ma'am, why is it cooler on top of a mountain?"

Ma'am replied - "We have to first know about our atmosphere to understand why it is cooler on mountain tops. In our atmosphere, there are three layers. Each layer is different from the other. The bottom layer which is about 16 Km high, is the troposphere. In the troposphere, most of the weather takes shape. The second layer of air is the stratosphere which is above 16 km to a height 48 km. The top layer is the ionoshpere. These layers form a blanket several hundred kilometres thick.

In the troposphere, the temperature drops steadily as we go up. For each 300 metres, the temperature drops about 2 degrees centigrade. A mountain which is about 1.5 km high will be 8 degrees cooler at the top. You can well imagine how cool the top of the Mount Everest would be which is 8,848 metres high. If we go to the top of the troposphere, we would have to bear with a temperature which is nearly 60 degrees below zero!"

Is the south pole as cold as the north pole?

Ragini asked - "Ma'am, Is the South Pole as cold as the North pole?"

Ma'am replied - "In fact, the climate in the South Pole is much more severe than in the North Pole. It is the Continent of Antarctica which the South Pole area consists of. It is a huge area, twice as large as the USA. This is the place where Penguins live without any fear of being caught by any other animal. The South Pole region is separated from all other continents, except of course South America, by hundreds of miles of Oceans. It has no local population nor are there any land animals except Penguins. The plant life is very scarce. The only things that grow there are lichens, mosses, grasses and a few flowering plants. In Antarctica, a huge icecap spreads over most of it and in summer also, the average temperature is below freezing. And in winter, the temperature is -23 to -35 degrees centigrade!

The North Pole region is completely different from the South Pole. Here is the Arctic Ocean surrounded by the margins of North America, Europe and Asia."

How are icebergs formed?

John asked - "Ma'am, how are icebergs formed?"

Ma'am replied - "An iceberg is a piece of glacier. The glaciers are like rivers of ice. There are places where the snow can't melt due to the temperature which does not rise above the freezing point. The snow turns into ice and a lot of ice eventually form a glacier. The glacier starts sliding down the slope like a great river and push down valleys until it reaches the sea. There it breaks off and the pieces form floating icebergs."

John - "Do all the glaciers reach the sea?"

Ma'am replied - "No, they don't. Some times they end in deep steep sided valleys called "fiords". From these "fiords", the icebergs float down to the ocean. Some icebergs measure over 100 metres and some of them even 1000 metres across. There are some small icebergs which measures only 5 to 10 metres and the seamen call them "growlers". Some of the giant icebergs weigh as much as 180,000,000 tonnes!"

Where are the biggest glaciers?

Sanjana asked - "Ma'am, the biggest glaciers must be in Antarctic, aren't they?"

Ma'am replied - "Most glaciers are in Antarctic and Greenland but the biggest glaciers are in Iceland which is an island covering 103,000 square kilometres.

VATNO JOKULL, the world's largest glacier has an area of 8,800 square kilometres and is 150 kilometres long. HOFSJOKULL, the 6th biggest at 1350 square kilometres and 36 kilometres long. LONGJOKULL, the 8th biggest has an area of 1300 square km and a length of 55 km.

The second largest glacier is at Malaspina, Alaska, which covers an area of 3,800 square km. It is followed by Russia's NOVAJA ZEMLJA with 3,000 square km.

In Europe, the highest mountain range is the Alps, with a total of 500 square km of glaciers. And of these, the ALETSCH glacier is the biggest with its 38 km of length."

Are the seashells skeletons of sea creatures?

Sanjeev said - "Ma'am, in Puri I was so happy to see hundreds of shells lying on the sea beach. Along with my parents I collected seashells which I still have. How are seashells formed?"

Ma'am replied "The seashells are actually the skeletons of many sea creatures. The molluscs have shells outside their soft bodies. The shell is its skeleton. The molluscs are the soft bodied but hard shelled animals

like snails, oysters. The shells are a part of them and they are attached to the shells by the muscles. They can never leave the shells."

Sanjeev asked - "What is the shell made of?"

Ma'am replied - "It is made of a form of limestone. And this limestone is built by the mollusc itself. The mollusc has certain glands in its body which helps it to take limestone from the water and deposit it in the particles at the edge of, and along the inside of the shell. As a mollusc (snails and oysters) grows in size, its shells increases in size and thickness."

Sanjeev said - "Some shells have beautiful colours!"

Ma'am replied - "There are some glands in the mollusc which contain colouring matter. With the help of this matter the mollusc colours its shells. When they die, these shells lie in the sea beach and wait to be picked up by some one."

Why is the seabeach full of sand?

Nitya asked - "Ma'am., Why is the seabeach full of sand?" And how is sand formed?

Ma'am replied - "A solid rock breaks up into smaller particles when it is exposed to wind, rain and frost. These particles which are very small, between 0.05 millimetres and 2.5 millimetres in diameter, are called "sand".

In the sea beach, the rocks are always exposed to the tides and the wind blown sand constantly rub against them. Moreover the salt water also dissolve some of the minerals in the rocks. All these combine to make sand. And that is the reason why the seabeach is full of sand."

What is plankton?

Monica asked - "Ma'am,, what is meant by plankton?"

Ma'am replied - "The plankton is a drifting mass of life. It is made up of billions of tiny living creatures. The word plankton is from the Greek word for "wandering" or "drifting". Some of the organisms that make up plankton, such as tiny green plants, always remain plankton. But others such as fishes and lobsters are plankton only while they are very young. All planktons drift in the sea water. They can not move on their own neither do they have the strength to move against the current. It is the tide or wind which carry them along."

"The molluscs are part of the plankton at the first stage of their life. Plankton includes eggs and larvae of many fishes."

"Plankton drift among the sea coast because it is in the sea coast where they find mineral water and light which they need for their survival."

Is the equator hottest place on the earth?

Rohit asked - "Ma'am, which place is the hottest on earth?"

Ma'am replied - "It's the equator. You all know that the surface of the earth is curved. The rays from the sun strike the earth vertically at the equator. That is the reason the heating effect of the sun is the greatest at the equator. And it is the least at the poles. The rays strike the earth at the angle above and below at the equatorial region. This means the regions above and below the equator. The temperate zones

19

receive, fewer rays from the sun than the areas in the region of the equator, the tropical zone.

What happens when a ray of sunlight strikes the earth at an angle? It has to pass through more atmosphere and therefore some of its heat is absorbed by the air. This is the reason the other zones receive less heat."

Why is the center of the earth hot?

Sashank asked -"Ma'am, why is the center of the earth is hot?"

Ma'am replied -"To understand why the center of the earth is hot, we have to know about the earth itself, its structure. There are three main layers which the earth is made up of. The layers are the *crust*, the *mantle*, and the *core*. The topmost layer is the crust, which is made of solid rock and is about 30 to 50 km thick under the continents. The next layer, the mantle below the crust, is about 2900 km in depth. It is also made of solid rock. The core is the innermost part of the earth and it is 3,380 km in radius. The material of the core is liquid due to the great heat.

The earth in its origin was a ball of gas and dust. Some of the gas flowed away into the space. But dust collected due to the force of gravity and became the solid earth. In this solid dust were trapped radioactive elements. A radioactive element continuously breaks down and produces heat. The dust inside the earth began to melt. The molten material when came to the surface, lost heat to the surrounding space and after being solidified made the earth's crust. But beneath this crust, the earth remained very hot because the heat, which was produced by radioactive elements, never escaped."

What is an earthquake belt?

Mridul asked - "Ma'am, what is an Earthquake?"

Ma'am replied - "The crust of the earth is not the same everywhere. In some regions, the crust has not quite settled down firmly and there is a "fault". A "fault" is a break in the rocks of the earth's crust. Where the break exists, one rock mass rubs against another with great force and friction. The energy of this rubbing is changed to vibrations in the rocks. Earthquakes are the vibrations of the earth's surface."

Mridul asked - "Where do the earthquakes occur?"

Ma'am replied - "The areas where they occur are called "belts". The most important belt is the rim of the pacific ocean where most of the world's earthquakes have occurred. The earthquake belt begins at the southern tip of Chile, reaches up the Pacific Coast of South America to Central America, runs along the Mexican Coast to California and on to Alaska.

From Alaska, the belt continues to Kamchatka. Passing through the Kurile islands and the Aleutian islands, it stretches on to Japan, the Philipines, Indonesia, New Guinea, through various South Pacific islands. Another earthquake belt branches off from Japan and runs through China, India, Iran, Turkey, Greece and the Mediterranean."

What were the worse earthquakes?

Rajan enquired - "Ma'am, will you tell us about some of the worse earthquakes?" Ma'am replied -"The single region of the earth that has the most frequent earthquakes is Japan. There is an earthquake there almost everyday of the year! But of course most of these are minor earthquakes and do not damage at all.

The Tokyo Quake of 1923 had killed more than 100 thousand persons and destroyed the city of Yokohama! The Chinese Quake in 1920 covered more than three hundred square miles and killed about two hundred thousand people.

In one of the worst earthquakes of Europe, in Portugal, the city of Lisbon was destroyed and almost thirty thousand people were killed in 1755. In North America in the San Francisco the earthquake of 1906, a great fire followed the quake and seven hundred people died and immense property was damaged.

The greatest earthquake on record in the USA is hardly known to most people because the area was sparsely settled and not much damage was done. It took place near the town of New Madrid, Missouri, in 1811 and 1812. There were 1,874 separate earthquake shocks felt and some of the shocks were felt four hundred miles away."

Why do volcanoes appear?

Mohini asked -"Why do volcanoes appear?

Ma'am replied -"The earth's crust in certain areas are weak and so volcanoes appear. What is a volcano? We all know that the center of the earth is very hot. The deeper its the earth, the higher the temperature. At a depth of 20 miles, it is 1000 to 1,100 degrees centigrade and so most rocks melt.

Lava is the molten rocks mixed with steam and gas. Lava is forced out of the interior of the earth through cracks in the solid surface. The eruption is really a gas explosion but some of the lava becomes finely powdered and makes the eruption look like black smoke.

The city of Pompeii, a Roman city in Italy was buried completely under the flow of lava from the famous volcano, Mount Vesuvins, two thousand years ·ago."

Mohini asked - "Where do volcanoes appear the most?"

Ma'am replied - "Central America, bordering the Pacific Ocean, is one of the most active volcano areas of the world."

How are caves formed?

John asked - "Ma'am, how are caves formed?

Ma'am replied - "Caves are formed in many different ways. When sea waves beat against the rocks constantly, hollows appear and in course of time, they are turned into caves. There are caves which are formed under the surface of the earth. These are usually the old courses of underground streams which have worn away layers of the soft rocks. Many caves were formed due to the volcanoes. When a volcano occurs, many rocks shift and leave behind caves.

The most common type of cave is made by the wearing away of thick layers of limestone. This is done by the action of water which contains carbon-dioxide. In places where there are great beds of limestone with an average thickness of 53 metres, such caves are many.

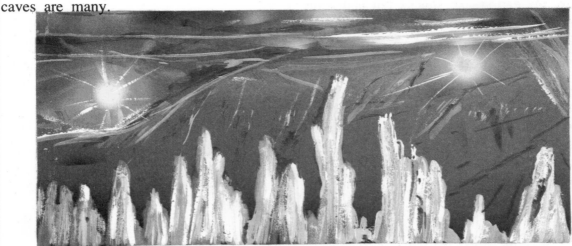

Some caves have galleries in tiers or rows, one above another. Some caves have openings through their roofs called "sink holes."

What are stalactite and stalagmite?

Arnab asked - "Ma'am, in some caves, there are icicle like things which hang from the ceiling and there are candle like things which cover the floor, What are they?"

Ma'am replied - "The icicle like thing is a stalactite and the candle like thing is a stalagmite. What are stalactite and stalagmite? How are they formed?

You all know that the most common type of cave is made by the wearing away of thick layers of limestone. Limestone is a soft rock which gets dissolved by a weak acid. The acid that dissolves limestone comes from rainwater. Falling drops of rain pick up carbon dioxide from the air and from the soil. This carbon dioxide changes the rainwater into carbonic acid.

A single drop of rainwater cling to the ceiling of the cave, about one million years ago. As the water dripped, a tiny ring of lime crystallized on the ceiling. A second drop and a third, fourth and fifth left lime in the same place. As time passed, the rings of lime formed a little stone "icicle", which **kept on growing. This** is called stalactite.

How was stalagmite formed? A drop of water dripped to the floor of the cave. Again the lime was left behind. Thousands of drops fell on the same spot, and the specks of lime formed looked like a stone "candle", which kept on growing. The "candle" on the floor is called a Stalagmite.

Some of them grow 2 cms a year while others take one hundred years or so to grow that much."

How are lakes formed?

Parikshit asked -"Ma'am, how are lakes formed? Are they always formed by rain water?"

Ma'am replied -"It is true that lake water comes largely from rainfall and melting snow but there are lakes which get their water from brooks, streams, underground springs, ground water.

What are lakes? Lakes are inland bodies of water that occupy depressions in the surface of the land. These depressions are called basins. These basins are formed in many ways. They may be the result of a fault in the earth's crust. They may be created by volcanoes. Sometimes the crater of an extinct volcano fills with water. Crater lake in southern Oregon is an example of this. Many lakes basins are formed by glacial erosion. All the great lakes (except Lake Superior and Lake Winnipeg in Canada) are examples of lakes that are formed by the glaciers."

What is hard water?

Sahana asked - "Ma'am what makes the water "hard"? How can we make out that the water is hard?"

Ma'am replied -"Hard water does not produce a soap lather easily. And when you boil hard water, it leaves a lime coating on the inside of kettles. This is the way you can make out hard water from normal water.

You all know that water is a compound of two gases - hydrogen and oxygen. But water is never pure, in its true sense. It contains dissolved mineral material, dissolved gases and living organisms. All these add a slight taste to water. Otherwise, chemically pure water is tasteless.

When raindrops fall through the atmosphere, they absorb some of the gases through which they pass. Most important of these gases is oxygen which makes it possible for living things to exist under water. Carbon dioxide is another important gas in water. Due to its presence in a water solution (carbonic acid), the water is capable of eroding

Where are bighorn sheep found?

HOW OTHER
CREATURES LIVE?

How can cacti live without water?

Is hippopotamus a relative of the pigs?

Priya said - "Ma'am , when I was a child, we had gone to see the zoo in Calcutta. And there, I saw a hippopotamus for the first time. I had thought it was a big pig and I was shouting out in great excitement - "Look at this pig, how big it is."

Ma'am smiled - "You will be happy to know that the hippopotamus is a distant relative of the pigs."
Priya asked - "Is it ma'am? No wonder they look alike. It had opened its mouth and we could see his teeth. Such long tusk like canine teeth!"

Ma'am replied - "The male hippopotamus use those teeth for fighting. Otherwise a hippo is a plant eater. They eat grass and chew it up with large grinding teeth."

Aditya asked - "A hippopotamus loves to be in water. Ma'am what is meant by "Hippopotamus"?

Ma'am replied - It means "river horse". It lies in a slow moving river during the day. Have you seen how its eyes and ears are placed? They are placed near the top of its head so that as much of its body as possible can remain under water."

Priya asked - Doesn't water go inside its nostrils?

Ma'am replied - "When it goes fully underwater, it closes its nostrils. And then at night hippopotamus leaves the river and goes

to the feeding ground to eat grass."
Aditya asked - "Where is the hippo found?
Ma'am replied - "The hippopotamus is found only in Africa."

Where are bighorn sheep found?

Akash said - Ma'am, I saw a movie on T. V. in which they showed sheep with big horns.
I have never seen such big horns on the sheep in real life."
Ma'am said - Those are called Bighorn sheep.

They are found in the Rocky Mountains of North America. Many animals live in the rocky mountains. And these animals are very tough. The life in the rocky mountains has made them tough."

Akash said - "Those Bighorn Sheep were climbing down the mountains as if they were walking on the land. They found no difficulties and none of them stumbled over the rocks.!"

Ma'am said - "Bighorn sheep are sure footed and they scramble among the rocks with ease."

Asha said - "We should have been sure footed like Bighorn Sheep. If we were, we would have climbed all the rocky mountains."

Why does the orangutan have huge throat pouches?

Romilla asked - "Ma'am, the orangutans have such huge throat pouches, it seems they have mumps! Why do they have such big pouches?"

Ma'am replied - "The orangutan use their huge throat pouches to make loud booming sounds while swinging from one branch to the other. The adult males live alone for most of the time. And the females orangutans travel in small groups with their young. Through those loud sounds they communicate to each other."

Romilla asked - "What does orangutan mean?"

Ma'am replied - "It means "man of the wood". The orangutans are quite like us. Like us, they can be identified by their facial features and expressions. But of course, the chimpanzee and gorilla are more closely related to us."

Nitish asked - "Ma'am are they found in all the forests?"

Ma'am replied - "No, they are not. They are found only in the rain forests of Sumatra and Barneo.

Long time back, they were found in South East Asia but its very sad that they are no longer there. First of all, the rainforests are being cleared away. And secondly, the young orangutans are caught for zoos."

Why does the kangaroo have a pouch?

Ma'am asked - "Can you tell me why does the kangaroo has a pouch?"

Shubho replied - "The kangaroo has a pouch to carry her baby with her."

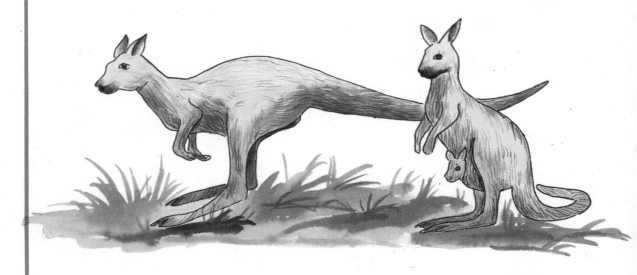

Ma'am said - "That's right. The kangaroo has a pouch between her hindlegs which is fur lined and which keeps the baby warm and safe."

Riya asked - "How small is the baby of a kangaroo?

Ma'am replied -"It's very small, not much over 3 millimetres. It's pink and is as thick as a lead pencil."

Shubho asked - "Ma'am, for how many

months, the kangaroo carries her baby in the pouch.?"

Ma'am replied - "For six months, the kangaroo carries her baby in the pouch. And when in six months, it grows as large as a puppy, the mother lets the baby out. But when there is danger, the mother hops over it, picks it up in her mouth and dropping it safely into her pouch, runs off."

Riya asked - "Ma'am, how many kinds of kangaroos are there?"

Ma'am replied - "There are more than 120 different kinds of kangaroos. The smallest is wallaby which is only 0.6 metres high while the biggest is the great red or grey kangaroo which is about 1.8 metres."

Why does a snake's tongue flicker in and out?

Mayur asked - "Ma'am that day a snake charmer came with a long snake around his neck. The snake kept on flickering its tongue in and out and it was staring at me! I thought the snake wanted to taste me!"

Ma'am smiled - No, the snake wanted to taste the air. A snake "tastes" the air by using a special organ in its mouth. It uses its flickering tongue to carry a stream of air samples back to this organ."

Mayur asked - "What is this organ called?"

Ma'am replied - "It's called jacobson's organs. This organ helps a snake's sense of smell. The jacobson's organs are sensory sacs that lie side by side and open into the roof of the mouth.

When the snake's forked tongue flicks out of the mouth, it picks up chemical particles from the air. And then the tips of the tongue are pushed into the jacobson's organs which taste the chemicals."

Where do the frogs go in winter?

Nidhi asked - "Ma'am, how does a frog breathe in?

Ma'am replied - "An adult frog sucks air into its mouth through two nostrils, at the same time lowering its throat. Then the nostrils are closed and the frog lifts its throat and pushes the air into its lungs. The way we breathe air into our lungs is different from that of the frog."

Nidhi asked - "Ma'am, its very strange that in winter, we don't get to hear the croaking of frogs. Where do they go in winter?"

Ma'am replied - "In winter they dive

into ponds, bury themselves in the mud and stay there all winter. Sometimes, the frog spends the winter in a hole in a soft bank. There are times, when they bury themselves under loose stones and earth."

Rebeca asked - "But ma'am, how does it survive without oxygen?"

Ma'am replied - "A frog needs very little oxygen when it becomes cold. It's because it is burning little food. And what little the frog needs during the winter, it gets from the pond water through the skin."

Why do the robber crabs climb trees?

Shashank asked - "Ma'am, we had gone to Goa once and there I saw lots of crabs climbing up the coconut trees. Why do they climb trees?"

Ma'am replied - "That's a mystery. It's really very strange and unusual It was believed once that they climbed trees to dislodge coconuts so that they could crack upon them and could eat the flesh. But then it was found out that a robber crab cannot get inside a coconut. They of course eat the flesh of the coconut but only after the coconut have been broken by other animals."

Shashank asked - "What does a crab eat?"

Ma'am replied - "Its main food is dead animal matter which is being washed up on beaches."

Rashmi asked - "Ma'am, where do they stay?"

Ma'am replied - "Crabs are generally thought of as sea creatures but robber crabs and other land crabs prefer to live on land. And the robber crabs that are found in the islands in the Indian and Pacific Oceans love to spend their time up on the coconut trees. If a robber crab is left in water for more than a day, it will be drown."

Where does a lungfish go for its summer sleep?

Adil asked - "Ma'am, which fish dig a hole in the mud and spend months together there?"

Ma'am replied - "It's the Lungfish. In dry weather, when its stream dries up, a lungfish starts burrowing into the mud. And then, it goes out to a deep sleep called "summer sleep" which helps in survival."

Adil asked - "Doesn't a lungfish dry up without water?"

Ma'am replied - "It's very interesting to know how it does not dry up. Do you know what does it do? It produces mucus, it produces a large quantity of mucus which hardens into a cocoon. Inside that cocoon, a lungfish sleeps. And its this cocoon which does not let it dry up."

Raka asked - "Ma'am, how does it breathe?"

Ma'am replied - "It continues to get air through the hole at the top of the burrow. Its body processes slow down and more-over it lives by absorbing some of its own muscle tissue."

Adil asked - "For how long does it sleep?"

Ma'am replied - "Till it rains. When it starts raining, when the stream fills up again, the lungfishes float up. You will be surprised to know that in Africa, some lungfishes slept for almost four years, inside their cocoon in the mud.!"

Which fishes kill with electricity?

Ma'am asked - "Have you heard of fishes which kill with electricity?"

Sanjeev said - "Ma'am, is it electric cat fish?"

Ma'am said - "Yes, that's right. It's electric cat fish. There are other fishes also like electric rays and electric eel which use

electrical discharges to stun and capture other fish. They use their electricity to warn off enemies also."

Sanjeev asked - "Where do they get electricity from?"

Ma'am replied - "They get electricity from the electric organs of their body. In an electric catfish, the electric organ lies just under the skin and covers its body and part of the tail. An electric ray, which is found in the warmer parts of the Atlantic Ocean, has two separate electric organs, one on each side of the head. And in the electric eel of South America, the electric organ is in its tail."

Sanjeev asked - "Ma'am, how much electricity do they produce?"

Ma'am replied - "The electric rays produce about 50 volts. An electric catfish can produce 350 volts. And an electric eel, the most powerful of them, can produce 550 volts!"

Have you heard of a fish and a shrimp sharing a home?

Ma'am asked - "Have you heard of a fish and a shrimp sharing a home?"

Priya replied - "No, Ma'am. Please tell us about it."

Ma'am said - "Its such an interesting thing! The Alphens shrimps dig burrows in the sand. There is usually a pair of shrimps in each burrow. And the pair of shrimps share their home with a fish called Goby."

Neha asked - "Do they stay together in the hole or do they stay turn by turn?"

Ma'am replied - "During the night, both shrimps and goby rest in the burrow. And during the day, the goby waits just outside the burrow, guarding it from danger.

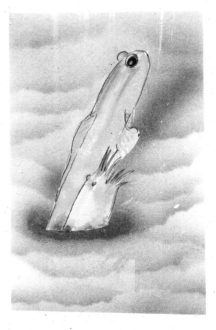

The shrimps never feed when goby is not around. Only when the goby guards their home they feed. And as a shrimp feeds, it keeps one antenna touching the goby's tail. If there is any kind of danger, the goby flicks its tails and they jump into the burrow and take shelter."

Aditya asked - "Ma'am, why doesn't the goby dig burrow?"

Ma'am said - "The goby can't dig. The shrimps can and so they provide the goby with a home. Shrimps senses are not sharp as the goby's. The goby in its turn provide them with a warning system."

Why do some fishes have no eyes?

Anand asked - "Ma'am, I saw the picture of fishes which have no eyes! Why don't they have eyes?"

Ma'am replied - "The fishes which have no eyes live in the caves under the water. In the caves, since there is no light, they do not need eyes. And since they do not use their eyes, they turn blind."

Anand asked - "Ma'am, are they blind from birth?"

Ma'am replied - "They begin life with normal eyes. But as they grow up and as they do not use their eyes, the eyes slowly get covered up with skin."

Shalini asked - "Ma'am, how do they find their way?"

Ma'am replied - "A fish finds its way by feeling the water, the pressure changes in the water. All fishes do this but a cave fish has got a very sharp sense to detect the pressure changes.

Some of the fishes also use their taste buds on their lips to explore their surroundings."

How do bats see in darkness?

Linda asked - "Ma'am, how do the bats see in darkness? Do they have very sharp eyes?"

Ma'am replied - "You will be surprised to know that the bats do not use their eyes when they fly in darkness. A bat makes a sound continuously while it flies. The sound waves strike the nearby objects and come back to its ears which are very sensitive. The bat then changes its course and avoids dashing against those objects."

Linda asked - "Why can't we hear those sounds?"

Ma'am replied - "The sound which a  bat makes is very high pitched. It's so high pitched that we can't hear it."

Linda asked - "Are the bats birds?"

Ma'am said - "Bats are not birds. They are mammals. Their youngs are born alive and they get milk from their mothers. They are the only mammals that fly."

Where do birds of paradise live?

Sanjeev asked - "Ma'am, In the picture book of birds, I saw some beautiful birds. They were full of colours and had lovely feathers! They were called "Birds of Paradise". Where do they live, Ma'am?"

Ma'am replied - "Birds of paradise are some of the world's most beautiful birds. They have lovely feathers which are in all types of colours - red, bright yellow, green and brown. Those birds are found in the forests of New Guinea. Do you know how many species are there? There are about 43 species of the birds of paradise.

Once upon a time, a crow like bird made its way to New Guinea from Asia. Its this bird that the bird of paradise has descended from."

Reshma asked - "Ma'am, they have got such lovely feathers. Are they being caught for that.?"

Ma'am replied - "It's very sad that thousands of these birds were being killed each year because their feathers were bought by the European hat makers.

But now, these birds are being protected."

What is a bird of prey?

Ragini asked - "Ma'am, what is a bird of prey?"

Ma'am explained and asked - "A bird of prey is the one which hunts live animals. A bird of prey has got sharp claws on its feet and has large hooked beaks. These help them in hunting live animals. Can you name some of the birds of prey?"

Ragini replied - "An eagle lives on animals and has sharp claws and hooked beak. It means an eagle is a bird of prey. Isn't it ma'am?"

Ma'am said - "Yes, it is. The harpy eagle which is the world's largest bird of prey lives on squirrels, monkeys and birds.

There are over 250 species of birds of prey. They include all the eagles, kites, hawks and falcons.

Some of the birds of prey live only on a particular kind of animal. The African fish eagle feeds only on fishes. The secretary bird in South America catches only reptiles. And one type of kites called everglades kites lives on freshwater snails."

What does the beak of a bird tell?

Mohit asked - "Ma'am, can you tell which food a bird likes to eat just by looking at it?"

Ma'am replied - "Yes, one can guess by looking at a bird's beak. It's the beak of a bird which tells us the kind of food the bird generally eats. The shape of the beak becomes different depending on the food the bird prefers to have. Birds of prey have hooked beaks. They need hooked beak to tear the flesh of the animal they have caught. Have you ever seen a picture of a heron?"

Neela replied - "Yes ma'am. I have seen a picture of a heron. The heron has a long beak."

Ma'am said - "That's right. The heron has got a dagger like beak so that it can spear fishes with it."

Mohit said - "Ma'am, a sparrow's beak is very small."

Ma'am said - "It's small but sharp. A sparrow uses it to eat seeds and insects. A finch which is a seed eating bird has got short cone shaped beaks."

Why are earthworms called the most important animals?

Neela asked - "Ma'am, why are the earthworms called the most important animals in the world?"

Ma'am replied - "It's because they prepare the soil for vegetation upon which our life depends?"

Neela asked - "How does it do it, ma'am?"

Ma'am replied - "The earthworm turns the soil over and breaks it by eating it. When it eats a dirt, it is pushed from the body as "casting". This cast contains lime

which makes the soil reach. The earthworms plant seeds. Do you know how is it done? When they take leaves in to their burrows, they pull fine seeds from the trees, which get planted below the surface."

Sruti asked - "Ma'am, how much soil pass through the bodies of the earth-worms?"

Ma'am replied - "In one year, the worms pass about 16 tonnes of soil through their

not only make the soil fertile, they also bodies in half a hectare of garden."

How do insects breathe?

Shubho asked - "Ma'am, how does an earthworm breathe?"

Ma'am replied - "An earthworm has got blood which carries oxygen from the skin to the internal organs and then it brings carbon dioxide out.

Do you know some insects breathe though they have no breathing organs at all? It's through the skins that the dissolved oxygen soaks in and the dissolved carbon dioxide soaks out."

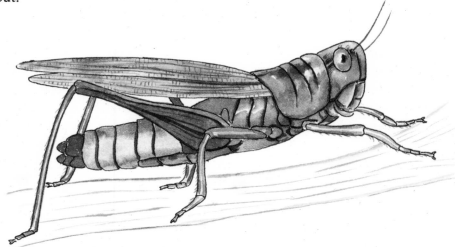

Shubho asked - "What is "Trachea"?"

Ma'am replied - "There is a tube called trachea inside an insect which works like our breathing tube or windpipe. If you look at an insect from close, you will see a large number of pores. Each of these pores is the entrance to the trachea. An insect may have hundred of windpipes in its belly to take in air. On the size of the creature depends how often air is taken in. The larger it is, the slower is the breathing rate."

Which insect lays 1000 eggs a day?

Meena asked - "Ma'am the number of termites increase by leap and bounds, don't they?"

Ma'am replied - "Yes, it's because a termite lays 1000 eggs a day!"

"A queen termite is a huge egg laying machine. It has a large bloated body,

up to 19 millimetres long which is the egg producing factory. She can produce over 30 eggs in a minute."

Meena asked - "When does she get time to feed herself?"

Ma'am replied - "She has to be fed by her worker termites, since she can't move. Termites live in big colonies. Some of their nests are huge towering ones. At the centre of the nest lies the queen with her smaller kings."

Asha asked - "Ma'am, when the queen termite is small, it does have wings, doesn't it?"

Ma'am replied - "Yes. A termite queen has wings but just before she starts laying eggs, her wings drop off. The king's wings also drop off. Together they find a new colony where she starts producing eggs. The queen may live for over 20 years!"

Why aren't spiders caught in their own webs?

Mayur asked - "Ma'am, when an insect gets caught in a spider's web, it just can't come out. Why doesn't a spider get caught in its own web?"

Ma'am replied - "If a spider gets caught in the web, it won't be able to come out. It will die in its own web. But a spider is well aware how to move around in the web. There is a sticky kind of silk which a spider uses to catch prey. But there is a non sticky kind which the spider uses to make the strong supporting spokes of the web. The spider avoids the sticky ones. It avoids the sticky ones by its sense of touch."

Mayur asked - "Where does the silk come from?"

Ma'am replied - "The spider gets the silk from its abdominal glands. The silk is forced through many tiny holes from the spinning organs at the tip of the abdomen. It comes out as a liquid which becomes solid when it comes in contact with air.

A spider produces many kinds of silk - the sticky silk, the strong non sticky silk and the silk of cocoon in which the eggs are laid. Some of these are soft and fluffy; others are hard and fibrous."

Why do mosquito bites itch?

Gurjeet asked - "Ma'am, there are so many mosquitoes in our house. And they keep on biting us. Why do mosquito bites itch?"

Ma'am - "My house is also full of mosquitoes now a days. It's the female mosquitoes which suck blood. The bill of the female has some sharp organs which are around a sucking tube. These organs are very piercing. When the mosquito bites, it injects a poisonous liquid into blood. It's this poisonous liquid which cause pain and itching and produces the swelling."

Gurjeet asked - "And they keep on humming. How do they hum, ma'am?"

Ma'am replied - 'They vibrate their wings rapidly and that makes the hum. The males make a deep, low hum while the female makes a shriller note."

When do wasps sting people?

Surinder said - "Ma'am, I feel afraid when I see a wasp. If it stings me, I will faint!"

Ma'am said - "Do you know when do wasps sting people? When they are being disturbed by them. If you stand still and let a wasp pass you; it won't sting you."

Surinder asked - "Do they kill other insects with their stings?"

Ma'am replied - "Yes, they do. Adult wasps feed on nectar and fruit but still they kill other insects. Do you know why? It's because their larvae feed on the bodies of the insects."

Surinder asked - "How do they feed their larvae?"

Ma'am said - "When they kill an insect with its sting, they take it to the nest and chew it up. And its juice is then fed to the larvae. Most of the wasps hunt other insects  like caterpillars. But there are some wasps which prey on the large spiders.

You will be surprised to know that a wasp's sting is its egg - laying organ."

Why do bees sting?

Mayur said - "Ma'am, whenever I see a bee, I just run off."

Ma'am smiled - "But a bee won't sting you unless and until you have harmed its nest. A bee stings to defend its nest."

Mayur asked - "Ma'am, is a bee's sting also an egg laying organ.?"

Ma'am replied - "Yes, it is. Its sting is shaped into needle like tube which is also used for injecting poison. A bee's sting has tiny barbs which sometimes are ripped out.

There are some ferocious bees. The giant honey bees of Asia are very dangerous and people have been stung to death."

Mayur asked - "Do all the bees sting?"

Ma'am replied - "There are infact thousands of different kinds of bees and many of them do not sting."

How does a caterpillar become a butterfly?"

Damini asked - "Ma'am, have you ever seen a caterpillar turning into a butterfly?"

Ma'am replied - "No, I haven't. I have always wanted to but I have always missed the chance. You never know the exact timing when it turns into a butterfly and flies away."

Damini asked - "Ma'am, how does a caterpillar become a butterfly?"

Ma'am replied - "From the eggs of the butterfly hatch out small wormlike grubs

called "caterpillar larvae". At once these tiny grubs begin to feed and grow and as they grow they shed their skins several times. They keep on eating and the food gets stored as fats. And this fat is later used to build up those lovely wings, the legs, the sucking tubes of the butterfly.

The caterpillar spins a little button of silk to which it clings. It hangs head down, sheds its caterpillar skin and then appears as a pupa which clings to the bottom of silk by a sharp spite at the end of its body.

The pupa may sleep for some weeks or months and then at last it emerges as a butterfly."

Why do crickets sing?

Shubho asked - "Ma'am, my mother said that in some countries like Italy, Japan and North Africa, people keep crickets in little cages because they love to listen to their songs."

Ma'am smiled - "That's very interesting. But the crickets actually doesn't sing. It makes its chirping noise by rubbing the ridged underside of one forewing against the surface of the other. And its the male cricket which does that. It's called "singing" because the sound is very pleasing."

Shubho asked - "Why do crickets sing?"

Ma'am replied - "The male cricket sings to call the female crickets. Crickets have very keen ears. You will be surprised to know that its ears are located on their legs and not on their heads!

I will tell you one more thing. In China cricket fight are held in which the crickets are set to fight with each other. And people who watch them sometimes bet on the outcome."

Which insects drink through straws?

Divya asked - "Ma'am, I've read some-where that there are some insects which drink through straws! Is it true, ma'am?"

Ma'am replied - "Yes. It is. Many insects do have straws for sucking up liquids. The straws are a part of their body. You all know about mosquitoes. They pierce the skin to suck up blood. Insects that suck up liquids have mouthparts that are extended into long tubes. A housefly has a tube with a sponge like organ on the end for sucking up liquid."

Divya asked "Does a butterfly have straws?"

Ma'am replied - "Yes, it does. A butterfly has got a long tube which it normally keeps coiled up and which is extended only when it is being used. There is a particular type of moth which has got a tube, 14 centimetres long to reach deep into certain kinds of flowers. You will be surprised that there is a South American moth which has got a straw, 30 centimetres long!"

It's being said that the best "Straws" are found in insects that drink nectar from flowers."

Why do some ants live in thorn bushes ?

Sashank asked - "Ants are found ev-erywhere, even in thorn bushes. Why do some ants live in thorn bushes?"

Ma'am replied - "In the whistling thorn bushes, you will notice large swollen bulbs at the bases of the thorns. The ants bore into these bulbs and digging out the material, build their nests inside.

The ants and the thorn bushes then help each other."

Sashank asked - "How do the ants helps these bushes?

Ma'am replied - "They help these thorn bushes by defending them from caterpillars and other insects. If an animal tries to eat the leaves of a whistling thorn, it is immediately attacked by a horde of biting ants."

Sashank said - "And how do the bushes help the ants?"

Ma'am replied - "The bushes provide homes to the ants. Not only home, but they provide food also. The tips of the leaves grow small "food bodies" which

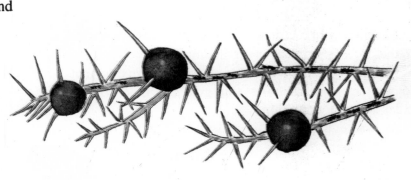

are being carried away by the ants. More-over the leaf stalks grow special nectaries from which the ants get a sugary drink."

Why do leafcutter ants cut leaves?

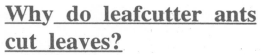

Aditya asked - "Ma'am, once I saw ants in the garden, carrying pieces of leaf which were much bigger then them! Why do those ants cut leaves?"

Ma'am replied - "Among the ants, there are "farmers". It's really such an interesting thing to watch these tiny leaf cutter ants carrying huge leaves to their nest. They cut up hun-

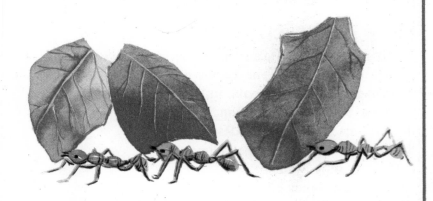

dreds of plant leaves and carry the pieces back to their nest. Once the leaves are inside the nest, hundreds of smaller ants come crawling and begin to chew those leaves. They keep on chewing up the leaves into a kind of compost. And this compost is being used to grow a special kind of fungus."

Aditya asked - "What with the fungus they do?"

Ma'am replied - "The fungus provides juicy branches on which the ants feed."

Aditya asked - "Does the fungus grow any where else."

Ma'am replied - "No, it does not. The ants look after it with great care. They feed the fungus with their droppings. And if any bacteria attacks the fungus, the ants use their saliva to kill off the bacteria.!"

Why do some plants lose their leaves in autumn?

Rohini asked - "In autumn, our garden is strewn with fallen leaves. Ma'am, why do the trees shed leaves in autumn?"

Ma'am replied - "These trees shed leaves so that they can survive the cold during the winter. In winter the soil gets too cold for the trees to take up enough water. Under normal conditions, plants waste a great deal of water. Water is taken up from the sap by the leaves and then given out to the air. But the trees know that they can't loose water during the winter when water is already scarce. To avoid loss of water in winter, they shed their leaves in autumn."

Rohini asked - "Why do leaves have different colours in the autumn?"

Ma'am replied - "Before the trees shed their leaves, they withdraw the chlorophyll due to which the leaves are green. When chlorophyll is no longer there, other pigments like yellow, red and orange give to the leaves other colours."

How can cacti live without water?

Johar asked - "Ma'am, how can cacti live without water?"

Ma'am replied - "The cactus does not live without water. It also needs water but it manages to survive with little water for long periods. Every living thing that has its home in the desert faces this problem - how to get along with very little water?

The cactus has no leaves. So what little water it has is not given out to the air. You will notice that its stems are formed in such a way that very little surface gets the direct rays of the sun. This is the reason why no moisture is given up. Its stems are thick to store water inside and the water is protected by the thick covering on the stem. No animal can drink

from it since there are scales on the plant. This is the way the cacti manage to live without much water. You will be surprised to know that some of the larger cacti plants can live for more than two years without water."

Have you heard of animal eating plants?

Nishi said - "Ma'am, I was so surprised when I came to know of plants which eat up insects! Why do they eat insects ?"

Ma'am replied - "There are plants which live in poor soil from which they don't get all the minerals they need to grow. So they have started eating up insects for their own survival."

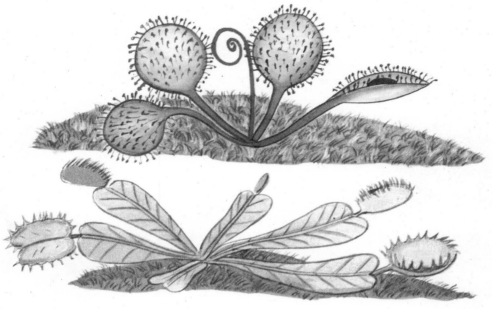

Mayur asked - "How do they catch insects."

Ma'am replied - "The sundews are insect eating plants. There are tentacles in their leaves and each tentacle has a drop of sticky fluid on the end. When an insect lands on the leaf, it gets glued to it. When it moves to get out, the other tentacles bend over it and traps it. And then the tentacles produce digestive enzymes which soon break down the soft parts of the insect. The plant then digests the insect and the tentacles open up to blow away the remains."

Sanjeev said - "Ma'am, I never knew there are plants which are non - vegetarians!"

How do we digest food?

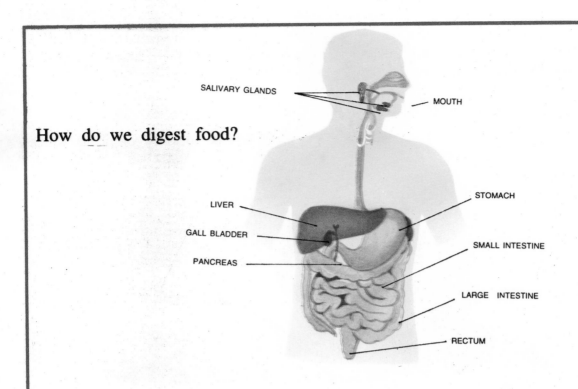

SALIVARY GLANDS

MOUTH

LIVER

STOMACH

GALL BLADDER

PANCREAS

SMALL INTESTINE

LARGE INTESTINE

RECTUM

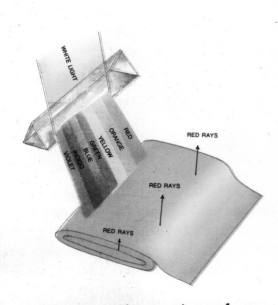

WHITE LIGHT

RED
ORANGE
YELLOW
GREEN
BLUE
INDIGO
VIOLET

RED RAYS

RED RAYS

RED RAYS

Why can't we see colours in the dark?

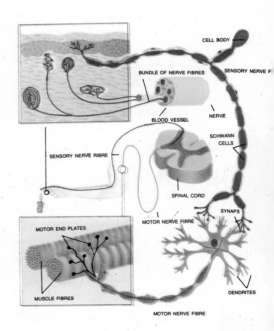

CELL BODY

SENSORY NERVE F

BUNDLE OF NERVE FIBRES

BLOOD VESSEL

NERVE

SENSORY NERVE RIBRE

SCHWANN CELLS

SPINAL CORD

SYNAPS

MOTOR NERVE FIBRE

MOTOR END PLATES

DENDRITES

MUSCLE FIBRES

MOTOR NERVE FIBRE

"What is a reflex action?"

What is a cold?

OUR BODY

What makes people sneeze?

Why do some people have brown eyes while others have black or blue?

Priya was observing everybody's eyes. When Ma'am came into the class room, she asked - "Ma'am, in our class, thirteen of us have got eyes which are black, eleven of us have brown eyes and one of us has got blue eyes. Why is it so?"

Ma'am replied - "Priya, you look like your mother don't you? You have inherited your mother's looks. In the same way, we inherit the colour of eyes from our parents, grandparents. We all carry two genes for each feature in our body. In most cases, one gene dominates the other.  In the case of eye colour, when both the parents have brown eyes, the children are going to have brown eyes. A brown eye gene dominates a blue eye gene. If a person has one brown eye gene and one blue eye gene, then the eyes are brown."

Rohit said - "But Ma'am, both my parents have got brown eyes and still I have blue eyes."

Ma'am replied - Some times a blue eye gene remains hidden but is not lost. It is passed on to the next generation. If one of your grandparents had blue eyes, the blue eye gene was carried and then passed on to you by your parents."

Rohit said - "That explains. My grandmother has got blue eyes."

How do we see colour?

Rohit asked - "Ma'am, how do we see colour?

Ma'am replied - "You will be surprised to know that it is actually the brain which "sees". When the image is brought to the brain, the brain cells have to interpret the image! It means we "see colour" in our brain. The brain has to receive images from the eye.

Our eyes are so constructed that they can perceive seven colours in the spectrum - red, orange, yellow, green, blue, indigo and violet. It's the cone cells in the centre of the eyes which pick up the wave length of the colour."

Meena asked - "What about the rod cells?"

Ma'am replied - "The rod cells which are on the edge of the retina can only distinguish brightness and darkness. It's being said that the eyes contain three sets of nerves which respond to the primary colours of light - red, green, blue - violet.

If all these sets of nerves are stimulated evenly, we see "white". If green light reaches our eyes, the "green" nerves are stimulated more than the others and we receive the sensation of green. This is the way we "see colour".

Why can't we see colours in the dark?

Meena asked - "Ma'am, why can't we see colours in the dark?"

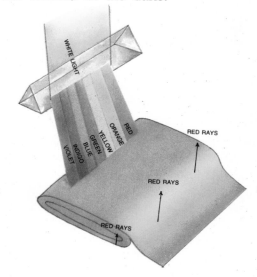

Ma'am replied - "Colour is actually a quality of light. All our colour sensations are caused by light rays which enter our eyes. How do we see object? All objects are seen by reflected light and the colours that they show exist in the light and not in the object. When you look at the sun, What do you see? You see white light, don't you? But white light is really a mixture of light of all colours, colours of the rainbow.

Mayur said - "Colours of the rainbow are red, orange, yellow, blue, green and violet."

Ma'am said - "Yes, when a beam of light is made to pass through a glass prism, we see all these colours. And colour is determined by the wavelength of the light. The shortest visible light waves are violet and the longest are red. When white light falls on an object, for example on a piece of red cloth, it absorbs all wavelengths except red. So we see the cloth as red.

That is the reason why we can not see the colour in the darkness. When there is no light , there is no colour."

Why do we have eyelashes, eyelids and eyebrows?

Mayur asked - Ma'am, why do we have eyelashes and eyelids?"

Ma'am replied - "Eyes are very delicate organs. They need protection. Eyelashes and eyelids protect our eyes. Eyelashes form two rows of stiff hairs around your eyes. If all of a sudden an insect comes closer to your eyes, it would not be able to come too close due to the eyelashes.

But if it comes too close to your eyes, your eyelids help you to close your eyes.

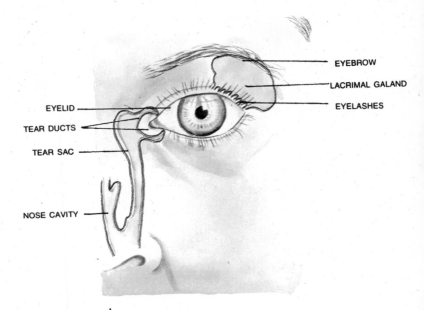

Your eyelids have muscles so that they can close. If there is a bright light, you close your eyes with the help of your eyelids and that saves your eyes from being injured. And when you blink, dust or dirt germs get removed."

Radhika asked - "Ma'am, why do we have eye brows?"

Ma'am replied - The eyebrows form two long patches of protective hairs above your eyes. It's the eyebrows which prevent moisture which flow down from your forehead from running down into your eyes."

What makes us cry?

Radhika asked - "Ma'am, do our tear glands produce tears constantly?"

Ma'am replied - "Yes, they do. They produce tears to bathe the front of our eyeballs."

Radhika asked - "Why don't tears overflow ?"

Ma'am replied - "They drain away, after bathing the front of our eyeballs. But there are times when the tear glands produce tears faster than they can drain away. For instance, when we are upset. Then they flow down our cheeks. It's the tearglands that make us cry."

Adit asked - "What is the main purpose of tears?"

Ma'am replied - "The main purpose is to defend the eye against outside infection. They have got a substance which kills bacteria. Tears are wiped over the eyes regularly by blinking. This is an automatic action which takes place atleast once every ten seconds."

Why do bruises go black and blue?

Adit asked - "Ma'am, when something strikes our body very hard, the bruises turn black and blue. Why is it so, ma'am?"

Ma'am replied - "When the blood vessels below your skin get damaged they release blood into your skin tissue which becomes purple in colour. The surface of your skin is tough compared to the tissues beneath it. So it is impossible to damage these tissues without breaking the skin. The damaged blood vessels release blood and the damaged cells also release fluid. And then the area becomes swollen with excess fluid."

Nishi asked - "How does the colour disappear?"

Ma'am replied - The blood that enters the skin tissues shows as a purple discoloration. After sometime, the blood cells break down and their contents are absorbed by the body again. When this goes on, the colour of the bruise changes to brown and then yellow before it disappears."

Why do people have different coloured skin?

Nishi asked - "Ma'am, some of us are dark, some of us fair, some of us have pinkish white skin others have yellowish skin, Why do we have different coloured skin ?"

CAUCASOID

NEGROID

EASTERN MONGOLOID

AMERICAN INDIAN

POLYNESIAN

Ma'am replied - "We inherit the colour of skin from our parents. The skin colour depends on a series of a chemical processes that take place in our body and the skin. There are colour ingredients in the skin. For instance my skin colour is black. It means my skin has more tiny granules of a substance called "Melalin", due to which I am dark. When there is yellow pigment in the skin, the skin is yellowish. The red colour of the blood, circulating in the tiny vessels of the skin also adds another tone to the skin. These four colours - white, yellow, black and red - are combined and by different combinations, we get different colours."

Robert said - "Why do many people lie in the sun?"

Ma'am replied - "It's because they want to get sun tanned. Sunlight creates melanin, the black pigment in the skin. When they spend a few days in the sun, the ultra - violet light of the skin creates more melalin in their skin."

What is the skin?

Robert asked - "Ma'am what is the skin?"

Ma'am replied - "The skin is an organ like the heart, the liver, the brain. Do you know that the skin is spread out over an area of 20,000 square centimetres! In each of these square centimetres, there are complicated structures ranging from sweatglands to nerves.

We have to remember that the skin has got two layers of tissue. One is a thicker deep layer called "corium" and on top of it is the delicate tissues called the "epidermis."

The epidermis does not contain blood vessels. It actually consists of cells that have died and been changed into "horn". We all are covered with horn shingles which protect us from pain."

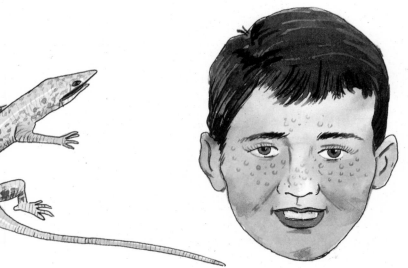

Linda asked - "Ma'am, how many layers of horn cells are there?"

Ma'am replied - "There are 30 layers of horn cells. Billions of the upper dead horn cells are removed every day in the natural course of our activities. But then billions of cells are being produced every day. The very bottom layer of the epidermis are very much active. They produce new cells. The new cells are pushed upward by the mother cells. Later, they are separated from their source of food and so they die to become horns."

Why do some peoples have freckles?

Linda asked - "Ma'am, my friend's brother has got a lot of freckles on his face. Why does he have freckles?"

Ma'am replied - "Will you tell me which is the pigment that makes us dark?"

Linda said - "It is MELANIN"

Ma'am replied - "That's right. Melanin is produced by a whole network of special cells. And these special cells are scattered through the lower layer of the epidermis. You all know that epidermis is the thin outer part of our skin. These special cells are called "MELANOCYTES". When these melanocytes cells bunch up in spots, freckles appears."

Linda said - "Ma'am, that's the reason why freckles have that brownish colour. It's the colour of the pigment melanin. But ma'am, why do some people have freckles?"

Ma'am replied - "It's heredity. We inherit it from our parents, grandparents."

What are touch and pain?

Gurjeet said - "Ma'am, why is it that my fingertips are more sensitive to the candle flame than the back of my arm?"

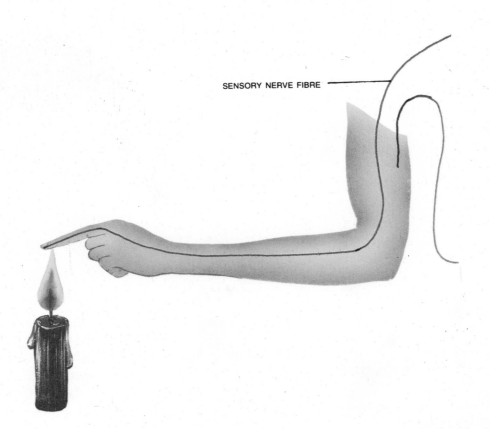

SENSORY NERVE FIBRE

Ma'am replied - "It's because in the fingertips touch receptors are plentiful.

Our skin contains many sense organs which are sensitive to touch, pressure, pain, cold and heat. These sense organs send information to the brain and tell the brain what is happening at any point on the skin. The touch receptors are nearer the surface of the skin. Cold and heat receptors are also nearer the surface. Pain receptors are free nerve endings. The pressure receptors are buried deep in the skin.

When you touch an object, more than one type of receptors are being stimulated. When you touch a candle flame, how many receptors do you stimulate?"

Gurjeet replied - "I stimulate touch receptors, heat receptors and pain receptors."

Ma'am said - "That's right, Touch receptors are more concentrated in the fingertips, the tip at the nose and the lips."

Why do we perspire?

Shubho asked - "Ma'am, why do we sweat so much while playing?"

Ma'am replied - "Sweating cools you down when you get too hot while playing. How does it happen? If we look at our body, it could be said that it is a permanent furnace. The food we take in is "fuel" which the body "burns up". About 2500 calories are being used everyday in the body. It's enough heat to bring 23 litres of water to the boiling point! But we know that our body heat remains at an average temperature of 37 degrees centigrade. How does it happen?

Our body temperature is controlled by a centre in the brain known as the temperature centre. There are three parts in it -a control centre, a heating centre and a cooling centre."

Shubho said - "Ma'am, is it the cooling centre which causes sweat?"

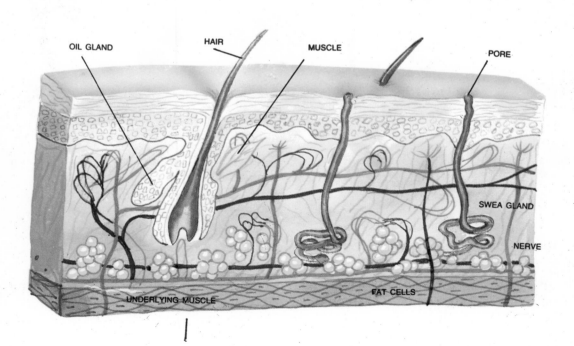

OIL GLAND HAIR MUSCLE PORE

SWEA GLAND

NERVE

UNDERLYING MUSCLE FAT CELLS

Ma'am replied - "That's right. When you are playing your body temperature gets too high. You need to loose heat. It's the cooling centre which goes to work. The sweat glands, which are on the surface of your skin, produce sweat. The vessels in the skin are opened so that the extra heat can radiate away and the sweat can evaporate and cool the body."

What is a reflex action?

Rohini asked - "Ma'am, what is exactly a reflex action?"

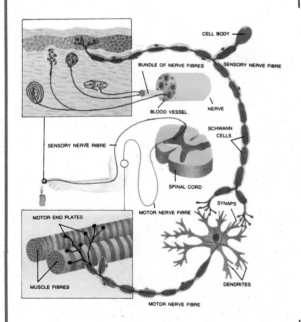

Ma'am replied - "If you place your finger unknowingly too close to a heater, you withdraw your hand immediately, without even thinking about it. This is reflex action. A reflex action is one that happens without the person thinking about it. When you put the heater away, so that no body gets burnt, it's your brain which is sending out instructions to your muscles. It means you are thinking. But in a reflex action, the brain is not directly involved."

Rohini asked - "Ma'am, if brain is not involved, then what is involved in reflex action?"

Ma'am replied - "It's the spinal cord. When your finger almost touched the heater the pain receptors in your fingers quickly send out impulses which travel to the spinal cord. From there, some impulses are relayed to the brain. But impulses are also sent directly from the spinal cord to your finger. And that's why you pull back your finger."

What makes people sneeze?

Sanjeev asked - "Ma'am, what makes people sneeze? And why can't we control our sneezes?"

Ma'am replied - "We cannot control our sneezes because it is a reflex act. A reflex action happens without our control.

When we sneeze, we send out air from the nose and mouth. Why do we sneeze? We sneeze when the nerve endings of the mucous membrane of the nose are irritated."

Sanjeev asked - "Ma'am, when are they irritated?"

Ma'am replied - "They may be irritated due to the swelling of the mucous membranes of the nose. This happens when we have a cold.

It may be due to the foreign bodies or dust that somehow get into our nose.

It may be due to an allergy. When we sneeze, we are trying to expel air to get rid of the irritating bodies."

What cause hiccoughs?

Priya asked - "Ma'am, that day I had such an attack of hiccoughs! I just could not stop and went on and on. Is it a reflex action?"

Ma'am replied - You can call it a reflex action. Vomiting is a very strong reflex action. Hiccoughs is considered a half hearted and ineffective effort to vomit!"

Priya asked - "What causes hiccoughs?"

Ma'am replied - "When hot food has irritated some passage inside, hiccoughs start.

Hiccoughs can also start when gas in the stomach presses upward against the diaphragm. The diaphragm is the muscular portion between the chest and the stomach. The diaphragm tightens and pulls air into the lungs. But air can't go through and we feel a "bump" at the moment the air is stopped.

So hiccoughs are a reflex action of the body trying to get food or gas out of the stomach. Thereby it irritates the diaphragm which in turn affects the passage of air in and out of the lungs. We feel the "bumps" and call them hiccoughs."

What causes headaches?

Namrata asked - "Ma'am, why do we have headaches?"

Ma'am replied - "The large veins and others in the brain that drain the surface of the brain are sensitive to pain. It is not the brain substance itself but the coverings of the brain and the arteries that are sensitive. When they "hurt" you have a headache."

Namrata said - "Ma'am, once I had a toothache. And then the ache spread to my head also."

Ma'am replied - "When your teeth ears and muscles hurt, the pain may spread to the brain area and cause a headache. If the muscles that are near the head and over the neck are contracted, this also can cause a headache."

Ranvir said - "When I am very hungry I get a headache. And when my mother doesn't take her morning tea, she gets a headache."

Ma'am replied - "What really happens in these cases is that the arteries in the skull are being enlarged and this produces a headache."

What causes cramp?

Akash asked - "Ma'am, sometimes I get a cramp which is very painful. What causes

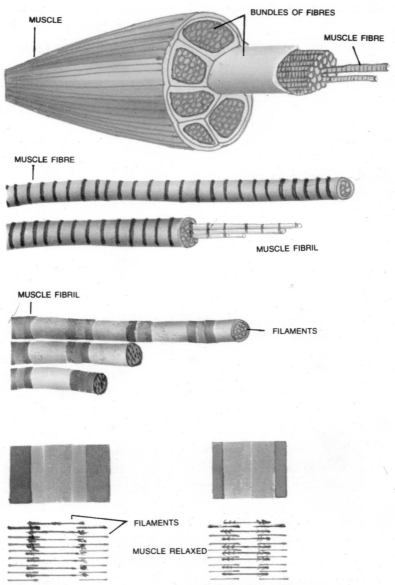

MUSCLE

BUNDLES OF FIBRES

MUSCLE FIBRE

MUSCLE FIBRE

MUSCLE FIBRIL

MUSCLE FIBRIL

FILAMENTS

FILAMENTS

MUSCLE RELAXED

MUSCLE CONTRACTED

a cramp?"

Ma'am replied - "It is often caused by lack of oxygen in the muscle. Cramp is a painful spasm of a muscle. By spasm is meant continuous contraction. When a muscle contracts, it uses up energy. During normal exercise, the body can take in sufficient oxygen. But the supply of oxygen may start to run out after a phase of too much of exercise.

At this point, energy is supplied to the muscle by breaking down the sugar into a chemical called lactic acid. A certain amount of lactic acid is not harmful. But if too much of lactic acid gets built up in the muscle, it causes cramp. Sometimes cramp may be caused by poor blood circulation."

Why does hair go grey?

Neha asked - "Ma'am, why does hair go grey?"

Ma'am replied - "In each hair, there are pigment containing cells which give colour to the person's hair. The cells in the hair follicle determine the colour of a single hair. The hair follicle is the bulb shaped structure at the hair root. What do these cells do? They inject pigment granules into the cells of the hair cortex. These pigment granules may be black, brown or yellow.

When these pigment producing cells in the hair follicles stop working, the hair that grow from these follicles become colourless. Due to the refraction of light, they appear white. White hairs mixed with black or brown hairs give an overall grey colour to a person's hair."

How do we taste things?

Sushank asked - "Ma'am, how do we taste things?"

Ma'am replied - "Our tongue is covered with tiny lumps which are called papillae. On the sides of some papillae, there are small groups of cells known as taste buds. Each taste bud contains four to twenty receptor cells, along with short sensory hairs. When you eat something, the mol-

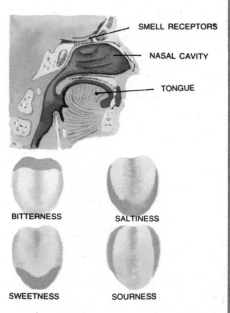

SMELL RECEPTORS

NASAL CAVITY

TONGUE

BITTERNESS   SALTINESS

SWEETNESS   SOURNESS

ecules of food get dissolved in your saliva. The taste buds in your tongue react to these dissolved food molecules. Can you tell me how many kinds of tastes are there.?"

Sushank replied - "Bitter, salty, sweet and sour."

Ma'am said - "That's right. Bitterness is tasted at the back of your tongue, sourness is tasted at the sides and sweetness is tasted at the front. And saltiness is tasted all over, especially at the tip of your tongue."

Vrinda said - "Ma'am, I think the taste

buds at the front of my tongue are the most active."

Why should we brush our teeth?

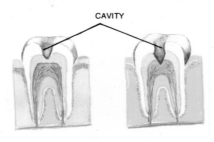

CAVITY

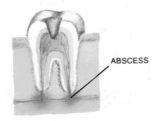

ABSCESS

Varinda said - "Ma'am, I am very fond of sweets. I don't feel like brushing my teeth after I have sweets."

Ma'am asked - "Tell me what will happen if you do not brush your teeth?"

Vrinda replied - When food molecules are left around our teeth, they form a hard material called plaque. Bacteria grow in plaque. These tiny living organisms thrive on any food that is left around the teeth. They grow in plaque and start to eat away the enamel layer of the teeth."

Ma'am said - "That's right. If this is not stopped, you will have a cavity. This cavity reaches into the inner pulp of the tooth. In that case, since nerve endings are exposed, you will have a painful toothache.

And if the bacteria infect the tooth right down to the root, then they will attack the bone in which the tooth is set. This causes an extremely painful abscess. Vrinda, now its your turn to decide whether to brush your teeth or not."

How do we digest food?

Akhilesh asked - "Ma'am, how do we digest food?

Ma'am replied - "Digestion starts in the mouth and stomach but most of it takes place in the small intestine. With the help of digestive juices which contain enzymes, digestion takes place. Enzymes are chemicals and these chemicals help to break down food.

When you put something into your mouth to eat, saliva mixes with it as you chew it. Then the food goes to the stomach where the food is being churned up for some time.

And the churned up food leaves the stomach gradually, a little at a time. In the small intestine, it is mixed with bile and digestive juices. The bile is being produced by the liver and stored in the gall bladder. And digestive juices flow from the pancreas. The enzymes break down proteins, carbohydrates and fats into simple chemicals which are then absorbed into the body.

The rest of the food passes into the

large intestine. Water is taken back into the body and the remains go to the rectum."

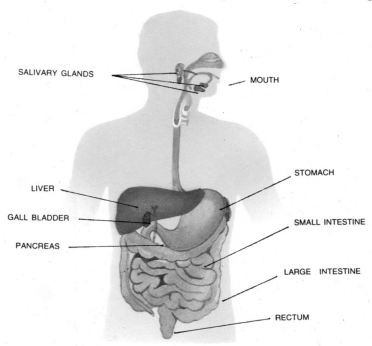

SALIVARY GLANDS

MOUTH

LIVER

GALL BLADDER

PANCREAS

STOMACH

SMALL INTESTINE

LARGE INTESTINE

RECTUM

What is a calorie?

Damini asked - "Ma'am, everybody talks about calories, everybody wants to control "calories". What is a calorie?"

Ma'am replied - "We often say that food is "burned" up like fuel. The way we measure the work a fuel does is by means of calories. A "gram calorie" is the amount of heat which is required to raise the temperature of one gram of water to one degree centigrade. The "large calorie" is 1,000 times as great. We generally use the large calorie to measure the energy value of food. Each type of food, as it "burns up", furnishes a certain number of calories. One gram of protein gives us four calories while one gram of fat gives us nine calories.

What happens when we take in more fuels than we need? The body uses up what it needs and stores some of it away for future use. But how much the body can store? It can store away about 1/3 of the amount it needs each day. What about the rest of the fuel? It becomes fat!"

Damini said - "Now I know why people say they have to cut down their calories!"

Why do we need salt?

Tripti asked - "Ma'am, our body contains 47 litres of water. Is it pure water?"

Ma'am replied - "No, it is not. It is actually a salt solution. Many of our organs have a high salt solution content. You will be surprised to know that the brain has 79 percent of it, the kidney has 83 percent, muscles contain 75 percent of the fluid while the liver has 70 percent!

Once upon a time, every life matter lived in the sea. The body fluid of these creatures was sea water. We have descended from them and so our body needs salt solution."

Tripri asked - "Ma'am, is it the reason why we have to take salt in with food?"

Ma'am said - "Yes, that's right. The land is not able to provide enough salt in a natural way. The plants which grow in the land do not contain enough salt. So we need to mix salt in our food before we take it in."

How do we smell things?

Nomit asked - "Ma'am, how do we smell things?

Ma'am replied - In the roof of the cavity of the nose, smell receptors are there. They have sensory hairs that branch and project into the mucus that lines the cavity. Molecules in the air dissolve in the mucus and stimulate these hairs."

Nomit asked - "Ma'am the sense of smell in a dog is much more than in us. Why is it so?"

Ma'am replied - "In our nose, the smelling area is about the size of a fingernail on each side. But in a dog, this area would cover more than the half the animal skin, if the membrane were spread out. Moreover in the human brain, where the sensations of smell "register", about a twentieth of the brain is concerned with smell. And in the case of a dog ? One third of a dog's brain is concerned with a sense of smell."

Prakash asked - "Ma'am, how many types of smell can our nose detect?"

Ma'am replied - "It's being said that there are 15 different kinds of smell receptors and they can detect over 10,000 smells!"

What is a cold?

Surya asked - "Ma'am, I keep on suffering from "cold". I'm fed up of my "running noses" and of my sneezes. And my throat gets sore too. What is a cold?"

Ma'am replied - "It is generally believed that the infection is caused by a virus of some kind. But you will be surprised to know that the virus is probably in our throat most of the time."

Surya asked - "Ma'am when does it attack us?"

Ma'am replied - "It attacks when our body resistance is low. There may also be other bacteria present and they don't attack either until your resistance is low."

Surya asked - "Ma'am, how does one keep resistance high?"

Ma'am replied - "You keep your resistance high with a good diet. Moreover you have to take plenty of rest and sleep also."

What is pain?

Divya asked - "Ma'am, what is pain? I wish I could feel no pain in my body."

Ma'am replied - "But Divya, we are lucky that we feel pain. Pain is our protector. If you didn't feel the pain at the toothache, you perhaps would not have taken care of it in time.

What is pain? It is believed that pain is due to an injury to the free nerve endings in the skin."

Divya asked - "Ma'am, what are "pain spots"?"

Ma'am replied - "Pain spots are the points on the skin which respond to stimuli with a sense of pain."

Divya asked - "Ma'am, are these pain spots spread all over the body ?"

Ma'am replied - "Yes, but they are not distributed equally. But on the average there is one pain spot for every part of the skin as big as this letter "O". There are about 3,000,000 spots on the skin where pain can be produced. Pains of all kinds - burning, cutting, gnawing, boring."

Why do we have April Fool's day?

What type of mirrors were first used?

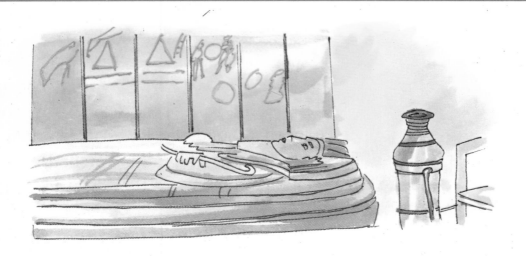

How did the egyptians preserve mummies?

How it began?

Why do we have christmas trees?

Where was the first theatre?

Jamini asked - "Ma'am, where was the first theatre?"

Ma'am replied - "It was in Greece where the first theatre developed. It began as a part of religious observance. At the foot of a hill, the worshippers danced around the alter of God while the spectators sat on the slope of the hill and watched.

The word "theatre" also came from Greece. By "theatre" , they meant "a place for seeing."

In 500 B. C., a theatre was built in Athens which had a circular place. The first permanent stone theatre was built in Rome in 52 B..C. It was the first time that theatre was filled with seats and the play was presented on a raised stage.

The first modern theatre was built in Italy in 1618. It was called TEATRO FARNESE."

When were museums started?

John asked - "Ma'am, when were museums started?

Ma'am replied - "In the 3rd century B.C., one of the first institution called to be a museum was founded in Alexandria in Egypt. In the museum, there were statues, elephant tusks, hides of unusual animals, instruments used in astronomy and surgery.

Between 3rd century B.C. and the 19th century there were many museums but since they belonged to princess and "noble families", common people could not even enter the museums.

It was only after the French Revolution, that the doors of French museums were opened to everyone. The Republican Government made the LOUVRE in Paris a national museum in 1793.

And in the 19th century, buildings were specially designed as museums for the first time."

How did the egyptians preserve mummies?

Ruhi asked - "Ma'am, how did the Egyptians preserve mummies?"

Ma'am replied - "Before 3000 B.C., the Egyptians buried their dead in the hot sand of the desert and it was sand which preserved the bodies. Later. they began to bury the dead bodies in the pyramids and in the rock tombs. But since these places were not dry as the sand, they thought of some other method.

The body was first treated with salts which took out the moisture. After the body dried out, it was bathed, rubbed with resin from pine trees and wrapped up in hundreds of yards of linen. They worked on the body for almost 70 days before they put it into the mummy case. The mummy case was put in a tomb the walls of which were decorated with pictures telling the story of the dead."

How did animals get their names?

Sanjeev asked - "Ma'am, what is meant by Rhinoceros, Giraffe?

Ma'am replied - "Rhinoceros came from Greek words - "Rhino" meaning the nose and "Keras" which means a horn. "Giraffe" came from the Arabic word "Zirafoh" which means "long neck."

It is very interesting to know how the animals got their names. Each name developed in a different way. "Leopard" came from the Latin word "leopardus" meaning a "spotted lion". "Hippopotamus" is from Greek words - "Hippos" meaning "horse" and "potamus" meaning "river". The duck is so named because this bird "ducks" in water. "Duck" is from an old English word "duce" meaning a "diver" The name "poodle" comes from the German "pudel" which is a short form of "pudelhund". By "pudelhund" is meant "a dog that splashes in water."

When did people begin to pierce their ears?

Nirja asked - "Ma'am, when did people begin to pierce their ears?"

Ma'am replied - "People began to pierce their ears to wear earrings in the prehistoric times. The ancient Persians, Indians, Egyptians, Arabians, they all wore earrings. The Greeks made beautiful gold earrings for the statues of their goddesses. And until the boys reached adolescence, they wore earrings.

The Romans also wore earrings. They even studded the earrings with pearls and jewels. Roman men also became very fond of wearing earrings and they all began to pierce their ears. It is said that in the 3rd century A.D., the Roman Emperor issued an order, forbidding men to pierce their ears!

After the middle ages men began to wear earrings in left ear only. When the hair style changed and hair was worn over the ears, the earrings went out of style. But in the 15th and 16th centuries, the earrings came back. In India, it was always there and never went out of fashion. Kings and Queens, both wore earrings. Now a days its only the women who get their ears pierced."

When did men start to shave?

Manish asked - "The pre historic men let their beards and hairs grow. When did they start shaving them off?"

Ma'am replied - "Shaving was started as a part of religious custom. At a certain point of time, they must have realized long beards and hair caused extreme inconvenience, since they gathered a whole lot of dust and dirt. Religion was associated with cleanliness too. So shaving became a part of religious custom. The ancient Indians, Egyptians did shave their faces for religious reasons. On the other hand the ancient Jews were required to wear full beards for religious reasons. To the Greeks, Alexander the Great, introduced shaving because quite often his soldiers were grabbed by their beards in the battlefield!

The early Romans did not shave until about 300 B.C. when barbers were introduced. And the Romans let their beards grow in time of mourning while the Greeks cut their beards, in times of mourning."

Who were the first barbers?

Radhika asked - "Who were the first barbers?"

Ma'am replied - "It is difficult to say who the first barbers were. In India, the barbers used to go to various households and cut their hair and beard. Their wives pierced the ears of women mostly in rich households. The first records of barbers in history go back to ancient Egypt. In ancient Greece and Rome, barbershops became favourite spots where men discussed various things.

Another interesting fact about the barbers of the ancient times was that they did surgery also. They treated wounds and even extracted teeth. In England, the king forbade the barbers to practice surgery in about 1540. Gradually, the work of the barber got separated from the surgeons.

The word "barber" comes from the Latin word "barba" which means "beard" Those days, trimming of beards may have been more important than cutting the hair."

What type of mirrors were first used?

Linda asked - "Ma'am, what type of mirrors were used first?"

Ma'am replied - "In the prehistoric times when people looked at their reflections in the river water or water pond, they must have got a shock. They did not know they were looking at themselves.! Gradually, they realised that a smooth surface reflects light and forms an image.

A surface has to be very smooth. And since then people have been trying out various methods to make a smooth surface. In ancient times, mirrors were made of polished metal. They were round pieces of metal brass, bronze, silver or gold.

The venitians were the first ones who began to make mirrors of glass backed with mercury and tin. It was in 1300 that they began to produce such mirrors and soon the glass mirrors replaced the metal ones."

When was copper first used?

Nikhil asked - "Which metal was used most in the earlier times."

Ma'am replied - "It was copper which was used by the people the most and from a very early time. You will be surprised to know that it was used even during the stone age.

Copper is found in fairly pure state. In the beginning, people got drawn to it because it looked very attractive. They must have picked up these red stones of metal and looked at them with curiosity.

Soon they discovered that these red stones of metal could be beaten into any shape. That was the most important discovery. Soon they began to make knives and weapons out of the copper. When they discovered that copper could be melted, they began to shape melted copper into cups and bowls.

Copper was the only workable metal known to human beings for thousands of years. When iron was discovered, the use of copper became less. Today, bronze (copper and tin) and brass (copper and zinc) are the two ways in which copper is being used. Beside iron and aluminum, copper is the metal most used in the whole world."

When were gems discovered?

Aditi asked - "Ma'am, when were Gems discovered?"

Ma'am replied - "Its not known when gems were discovered. But for thousands of years, gems were being worn by men and women in all the countries. Gems were valued not only as expensive stones but people believed that gems had the power to protect people from diseases and evil spirit. The Bible has mentioned Gems. In the 28th chapter, it was mentioned that high priest, Aaron, wore a breastplate which was studded with 12 precious stones."

Aditi asked - "There are different coloured gems, aren't there ma'am?"

Ma'am replied - "Yes. They were distinguished by their colours. All the stones of a red hue were called "Ruby". All green stones were called "emeralds" and blue ones were called "sapphires". Now a days diamonds are considered the most precious gems because they are the hardest of all stones."

Where did sugar originate?

Aditya asked - "Ma'am, where did sugar originate?"

Ma'am replied - "Sugar which comes from sugarcane originated in India. It was as early as 400 B.C. that cane sugar was used by all the people in India. When Alexander the Great came to India in 325 B.C., they saw sugarcane for the first time. One of the Europeans who came with Alexander the Great, said that he was amazed to see a grass which produced honey without the help of bees!

Between A.D. 500 and 700, sugarcane culture and sugar manufacture spread to Persia. And from there to Arabia, Syria, Palestine, Egypt.

In the USA, sugarcane was first introduced in 1751.

By 1795, the commercial production of sugar had begun."

Where did ice cream originate?

Avantika asked - "Ma'am, where did ice-cream come from? It must be from England, isn't it?"

Ma'am replied - "No, it wasn't from England. It was first made in East Asia.

Marco Polo the great explorer of Italy was the one who carried the idea from East Asia to Italy.

From Italy, it went to France. In France, the rich people tried to keep the recipes of ice-cream a secret so that common people could not have it! Such was the level of mean mindedness. But of course, it became known to all and it became very popular. And soon, it spread to other countries.

In 1851, the first wholesale factory for the manufacture of ice-cream was started in Baltimore, Maryland. And when refrigeration was invented, ice-creams became available in summers too."

Where was surfing first done?

Gyanesh asked - "Ma'am, surfing is such a wonderful sport. Where was it first done?"

Ma'am replied - "It was done in the Pacific Islands hundreds of years ago. In 1788 when Captain James Cook discovered Hawaii, he found surfing to be a popular sport among the people.

There, surfing contests were held. The boards which they used were

4 to 5 metres long and each board, weighed 68 kilograms!

A big change came over which made surfing very popular - the use of lightweight boards.

You all know surfing is the sport of riding ocean waves on a long narrow surfboard. The boards which are about 3 metres long and weigh as little as 10 kg, can be used by even children. That's the reason surfing has become such a popular sport now."

Where was the first lighthouse built?

Asha said - "Ma'am, I saw a lighthouse when I had gone to Gopalpur. At night, its light flashed around the sea beach."

Ma'am said - "When the first lighthouse were built, the towers were built low on which were kept metal baskets full of flaming wood or charcoal. Thousands of years ago, when human beings began to go out to sea in ships, they put up lighthouses so that the light would give them guidance, would warn them of dangers.

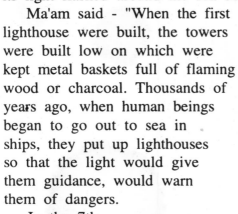

In the 7th century B.C. there was a well known lighthouse on Cape Sigeum at the Hellespont.

The most famous light house of ancient times was the marble pharas at Alexandria, Egypt. It was considered one of the seven wonders of the world. At its top blazed a bright fire which guided the ships into Alexandria from the 3rd century."

Where was established the first fire brigade?

Rehana asked - "Ma'am, how did people put out fire when there was no fire brigades?"

Ma'am replied - "In the olden times, when fire broke out, everyone became a fire fighter. They would form a chain and pass buckets of water hand to hand to pour on the flames.

It was in 1666 that the great fire burned down 13,000 buildings including St. Paul's Cathedral in London. After that incident, they developed hand operated pumps so that fire fighters could spray water through a hose. And then citizens volunteered to form companies and they promised to drop every kind of work and rush to fight fire wherever it broke out. They kept a paid bellman to patrol the streets at night to look out for fire and warn the citizen. Insurance Companies formed their own fire brigades but they fought fire only in those buildings which they had insured!

The first paid fire patrol was established in 1835 in the New York City. And in 1855, the first firehouse was organised in the city."

When was oil first used as fuel?

Abhimanyu asked - "Ma'am, when was oil first used as fuel?"

Ma'am replied - "That was in 1859. But let us understand where it is found. Petroleum which is crude oil, is found in rocks which are found deep in the earth. We try to reach the oil by drilling below the earth's surface. There are some places where petroleum comes out of the surface of the earth through cracks. The ancient people knew about this and they often used it in burning lamps.

It was in the 19th century that the Industrial Revolution brought the need for better lamp fuels to light the new factories.

George Bissel, a New York lawyer was the first man who thought of drilling for oil. He sent a sample of oil to Benjamin Silliman, a scientist. The scientist reported that petroleum led to many useful products: lamp oil, lubricating oil, paraffin wax for candle. Bissel struck oil in 1859 and that was the beginning of a phase of rush for oil. New uses for petroleum products were found, including its use as fuel."

How did the days of the week get their names?

Sharda asked - "Ma'am, why do we say Sunday, Monday...? How did the days of the week get their names?

Ma'am replied - "The names of the days of the week we got from the Anglo-Saxons. They called most of the days after their gods. The day of the SUN become SUNNANDAEG or Sunday. The day of MOON was called MONANDAEG or Monday. The day of MARS became the day of TIW, who was the God of war. This became TIWESDAEG or Tuesday. Wednesday from the God of WODEN. The day of the JUPITER, the thunderer, became the day of the Thunder God Thor, and this becomes Thursday. Friday was named after FRIGG, the Wife of God Odin. The day of Saturn becomes SAETERNSDAEG."

Why do we have April Fool's day?

Vikram asked - "Ma'am why do we have April Fool's day?"

Ma'am replied - "It is believed that in France the people celebrated the April Fool's day first. It so happened that in 1564, a new calendar was brought about and Charles IX ordered that the new year would begin on the 1st of January. Till then 1st April was the new year day. And with it was associated exchange of New Year's gifts. There were many people who still followed the old calendar and celebrated

the 1st April as the New Year day. Others made fun of them and started sending them mock gifts and called them April Fools. This is the way it started and then became the day when everybody tried to fool everybody else."

Why are eggs and rabbits associated with easter?

Shanti asked - "Ma'am, why are eggs and rabbits associated with Easter?"

Ma'am replied - "Both Easter and the coming of spring are the symbols of new life. Easter is the most joyous of Christian holidays because it is celebrated in com-memoration of the resurrection of Jesus Christ.

The egg is being considered as a symbol of fertility and new life. The ancient Egyptians and Persians celebrated their spring festival by colouring and eating eggs. The Christians also adopted the egg as a symbol of new life, the symbol of the resurrection.

In the legends of ancient Egypt, the hare is associated with the moon. If you look at the moon for a few minutes, you will see an impression of hare in it. The hare became a symbol of new period of life. The early Christians took it over and linked it with Easter - the holiday that symbolises new life. This is the way eggs and rabbits are associated with Easter - as symbol of new life."

Why do we have christmas trees?

Akash asked - "Ma'am, why do we have Christmas trees?"

Ma'am replied - "Trees symbolise life and people have always worshipped trees since the ancient times. Those trees which were evergreen were most respected. The Christmas tree was a custom and not a religious observance. The custom came from Germany. It was the Christians who changed the custom into one honoring Christ.

The northern people of Denmark, Sweden and Norway began to bring small trees into their homes at Christmas time.

To English homes, trees were brought by a German prince, Albert who married Queen Victoria. In 1841, Albert had the first decorated Christmas tree set up at Windsor Castle. Gradually the custom spread all over the world. And this is the way we have Christmas trees in Christmas."

What causes cement to harden?

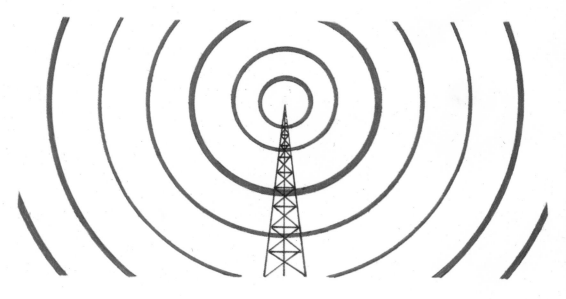

What are radio waves?

Why does swiss cheese have holes?

How things are made?

What is a detergent?

What causes cement to harden?

Shubho asked - "Ma'am, cement is such a soft powder by itself But when I added water to it, it became so hard that it would not dissolve in water! How is it so?"

Ma'am replied - "It is believed that the four compounds in the cement become crystals when water is added. These crystals interlock and therefore cement gets hardened.

Due to this reason, cement is one of the most useful materials in modern building. The kind of cement that hardens in water is called hydraulic cement. As early as the 2nd century B.C. the Romans had already discovered how to make hydraulic cement by mixing volcanic ash with lime.

Modern cement is made by heating a mixture of limestone and clay or slag to a very high temperature. This mixture is heated until large, glassy cinders - called "clinkers - are formed. The clinkers are then ground to soft powder, to which when you add water, it turns as hard as rocks."

How are bricks made?

Tarun asked - "Ma'am, how are bricks made?"

Ma'am replied - "Bricks are made of clay. Clay is found almost all over the earth's surface. You will notice that when clay is wet, it becomes slippery. And it can be easily moulded into any kind of shape. But when it becomes dry, it turns hard and stony. And after that even if you wet it, You cannot mould it. This is the reason bricks are being baked or burned at 870 to 1200 degrees centigrade. At about 535 degrees centigrade, the bricks turns red and its colour becomes darker as the temperature increases.

Bricks are one of the oldest permanent building materials. And over 5000 years ago, they were first used. Since the ancient times the manufacture of bricks has changed little except that now machines do most of the work.

You will be surprised to know that the average bricks can take a load of about 350 kilograms per square centimetre! Beyond that it of course gets crushed."

What things are made of oil?

Akash asked - "Ma'am, I was surprised when I came to know that kerosene, diesel are made from petroleum. What else is made from oil?"

Ma'am replied - "There are more than 2000 useful products which are made from petroleum or crude oil! This is done through a process called refining.

There are the high energy fuels which are petroleum products - petrol, kerosene, diesel and fuel oils.

There are over thousand different kinds of oils and greases which are made from petroleum. There are products of oil which are used in making carbon paper, ink to print books and newspapers. Our food and clothes depend on substance from oil. Moreover oil based sprays kill insects and weeds. Synthetic ammonia which is used as a fertilizer is made from petroleum.

Moreover petroleum is used to make petrochemicals from which other chemical products are made like plastics, synthetic foam rubber, plastic tiles and detergents.

The list of the products of the petroleum is a long one."

What is a detergent?

Nidhi asked - "What is exactly a detergent? We keep on hearing about it on T.V."

83

Ma'am replied - "Soap is one kind of detergent. A detergent is a substance which makes things clean. But a soap can be made from natural material like "reetha". But a detergent is made of synthetic materials.

What is there in the detergent which does the actual cleaning? It's called the surface active agent or surfactant.

This surfactant is made from petroleum, animal fats, vegetable oils. Surfactant is mixed with other chemicals which remove the dirt more thoroughly and doesn't let it come back.

Detergent has become very popular since it produces suds in all kinds of water - soft or hard, hot or cold."

How is synthetic rubber made?

Sanjeev asked - "Ma'am, natural rubber is made from the white fluid of rubber tree. But how is synthetic rubber made?"

Ma'am replied - "Synthetic rubber is made by people. The white fluid of rubber tree is called latex with which natural rubber is made. But human beings have learned to make latex by combining chemicals in certain ways.

To make synthetic rubber, butadiene and styrene are needed. Butadiene is a gas made from petroleum and styrene is a liquid made from petroleum or coal. The butadiene and styrene are pumped into a large tank containing a soapy mixture. Due to this soapy mixture, rubber particles are easily formed. A chemical is added and as the mixture is stirred it gradually changes to a milky white liquid. This is synthetic latex.

The latex is then pumped into another tank with acid and salt water. The mixture is stirred till it becomes semi solid. Its then washed and dried and then pressed into bales. "This is the way synthetic mixture rubbers are made."

How are synthetic fibres made?

Sudha asked - "Ma'am, we get cotton, wood, silk from plants and animals. But there are other fibres like rayon, nylon,. How are these synthetic fibres made?"

Ma'am replied - "To understand how synthetic fibres are made, we have to first know about fibres. Most fibres are made of chemicals, which contain carbon. In some of these chemicals, molecules attach themselves like the links of a chain. This is called POLYMERIZATION.

In making synthetic fibres, the chemists follow the same method. They take atoms of carbon, hydrogen, oxygen and other elements, and combine them in such a way that new substances are created. They take atoms from coal, oil, air and water and combine them, arrange them into long molecules which is called polymers. Instead of the nature, it is the chemist who creates polymerization. From the filaments of polymers, fabrics are made.

You will be surprised to know that of all the fibres produced every year, about 1/5 are synthetic fibres."

What is leather?

Meena asked - "Ma'am, what is leather? Is it made by people?"

Ma'am replied - "Leather is not made by people. It is an animal hide or skin which has been tanned by people. When we say "hide", we mean skin of large animals and when we say "skin", we mean skin of smaller animals.

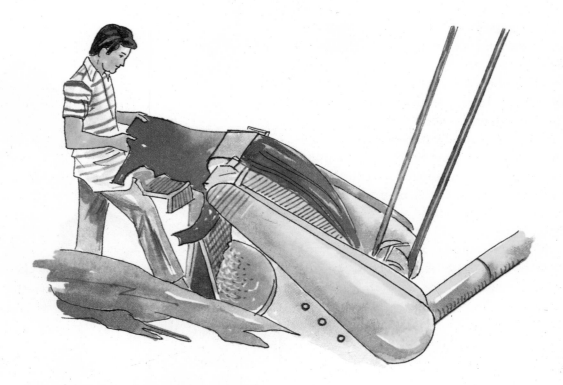

Cattle hide is used the most to make leather. Calf skin leather is much lighter than cattle hide but it is used to make the most expensive shoes and hand bags. Horse hide is used for shoes, jackets, sports equipments. The kangaroo hide is used for track and baseball shoes. Alligator leather and skins of snakes and lizards are used to make shoes, bags, luggage.

Animal hide and skins are turned into soft flexible leather by tanning, In tanning a bark called tannin is being used."

Meera said - "Ma'am, it's so sad that so many animals are being killed! I will rather use a bag made of cloth."

Why do golf balls have holes?

Ravish asked - "Ma'am, why do golf balls have holes? No other ball has got holes in them."

Ma'am replied - "If you look at a golf ball closely, you will see that they are not exactly holes. You can call them, "dimples". These dimples make the ball fly straight when it is struck properly. And these dimples lessen wind resistance. That is why these balls have greater carrying power. You must have noticed that a golf ball is about half the size of the baseball or tennis ball. A golf ball weights about 45.9 grams and its diameter is about 4.11 centimetres. Earlier, the balls used to be made of heavy leather and were stuffed with feathers. But now a days the ball is made by winding strip rubber tightly around a core and covering it with a hard rubber like composition material.

Due to the "dimples", the best players can hit a golf ball 275 metres or farther."

Why does swiss cheese have holes?

Archana asked - "Ma'am, Swiss cheese have holes in them unlike any other cheese. Why is it so?

Ma'am replied - "You must have noticed that Swiss cheese have a nutty flavour and are sweet. This is due to a special kind of bacteria called PROPIONI bacteria. The flavour of most cheese develops while it is curing. Curing takes place when the cheese is kept in storage in controlled conditions of temperature and moisture. During curing, harmless bacteria, yeast and moulds are allowed to grow in the cheese to give its flavour and odour.

In the case of Swiss cheese, the propioni bacteria gives off gas when it is curing. These gas bubbles form the round "holes" or "eyes" of the cheese. That is the reason the Swiss cheese have holes in them unlike any other cheese."

How is water made drinkable?

Nidhi asked - "Ma'am, when water is stored, it becomes drinkable, isn't it?"

Ma'am replied - "Yes. When it is stored in a reservoir, impure solid things settle at the bottom. This process is known a sedimentation. When water is kept in a storage, many bacteria lose their power.

But sedimentation always does not purify. CHLORINE is added to purify water. About two kilos of chlorine is added to nearly 4 million litres of water. Most of the dangerous bacteria get destroyed by this method. This method is very cheap, quick and effective.

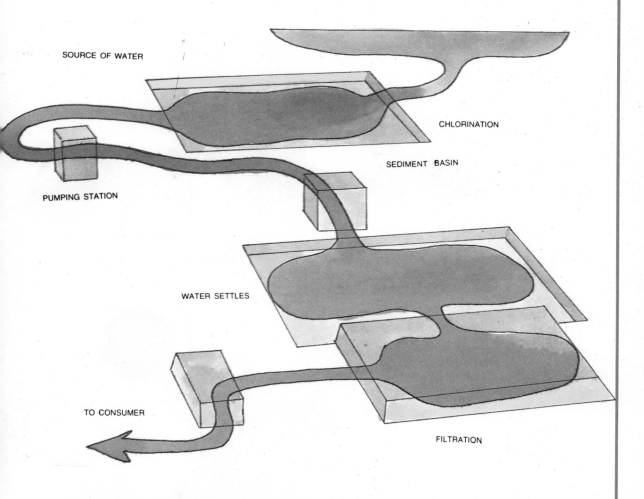

Another method is to filter the water through sand. Most of the bacteria and impurities get removed by this method.

Now a days there are water filters and aquaguards which make the water drinkable."

What is coal made of?

Koyal asked - "Ma'am, what is coal made of ?"

Ma'am replied - "Coals, which you see today, were trees and plants hundreds of millions of years ago! Coal is made of the remains of ancient trees and plants that grew in swampy jungles in warm moist climates. These trees and plants, when died, fell into the swamp water. They didn't rot because the swamp water protected them from rotting. Bacteria changed some of the wood to gases which then escaped. A black mixture, was left behind. This black mixture was mostly carbon.

Gradually thick layers of mud and sand gathered over it and squeezed out most of the liquid. A pasty mass was left behind which slowly hardened into coal

Can we make diamonds?

Rohini asked - "Ma'am how is diamond made?"

Ma'am replied - "The natural diamonds are found under the earth. The process of its production started about one hundred million years ago. That was the time when our earth was beginning to cool. There was a mass of hot liquid

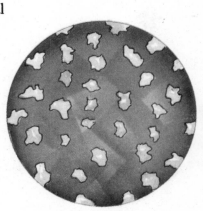

SYNTHETIC DIAMONDS

DIAMOND POWDER

LENS

INSTRUMENT FOR POLISHING LENSES

rock under the ground. Over this hot liquid rock, there was so much pressure and there was so much of heat that the carbon became crystallized. A diamond is a highly crystallized carbon. This is the hardest substance till now known to us."

Rohini asked - "Ma'am can we make diamonds?"

Ma'am replied - "People tried to make synthetic diamond. In 1954, the first synthetic diamonds were really produced. A special press was created in which carbon was subjected to a temperature of 2800 degrees centigrade and a pressure of 56,245 kilos per square cm. The first of these diamonds were yellow in colour and the largest of them measured just over 1.5 millimetres in length.

Someday perhaps somebody would make a perfect diamond."

Why does silver tarnish?

Rupak asked - "Ma'am, silver is the whitest of all metals. But it doesn't look as bright as it was in the beginning. Why does silver get blackened?"

Ma'am replied - "When silver is exposed to sulphur and many other sulphur compounds, it reacts very strongly and with sulphur and hydrogen sulphide, it forms black silver sulphide. This we notice as tarnishing of the silver ware. The sulphur is in the tiny amounts of sulfurated hydrogen, in air or it may be in certain food, like eggs.

Silver is found in nature as solid metal. But more often it is combined with other metals and non-metals in mineral ores. Pure silver is very soft. To make it strong and useful, other metals are added to it. Sterling silver is 92½ percent silver and 7½ percent copper.

Silver is very useful. It conducts electricity and heat better than any other metal. It reflects light better than other metals."

How are colours formed?

Uma asked - "Ma'am how are colours formed?"

Ma'am replied - "Colours are formed by the wavelength of light. Scientists think of light as travelling in waves. The distance from the crest of one wave of light to the next crest is called a wavelength. You will notice that the light from the sun or from any other hot source looks white. But actually this white light is a mixture of light of all colours. It's a mixture of many wavelengths. Each different wavelength produces a different colour."

Uma asked - ""How long are the wavelengths?"

Ma'am replied - "The wavelengths of light are so small that they are measured in millionths of a millimetre. The shortest visible waves are violet with a wavelength of about 0.0004318 millimetres. The longest are red, with a wavelength of about 0.0007112 millimetres.

Most of the colours are mixtures of many wavelengths. Purple is a mixture of red and violet, brown is a mixture of red and orange and yellow. A mixture of red and white is pink.

When white light falls on an object, some wavelengths of the light are reflected and the rest are absorbed by the material. For example, a piece of red cloth absorbs almost all the wavelengths except a certain range of red which are reflected to our eyes and we see red."

What is a laser beam?

Jyotish asked - "What is a laser beam? Why is it so strong?"

Ma'am replied - "A laser beam can take a weak beam of light and turn it into a strong beam. A laser amplifies light. It can produce such strong beams that when they are focussed, they can burn tiny holes in strips of steels in less than a second!

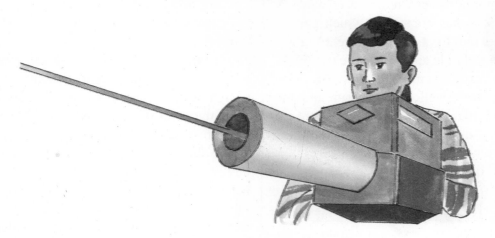

You all know that light from the sun or from a lamp is a mixture of many wavelengths. A laser beam is made up of rays that are exactly of the same wavelength. In ordinary light, light rays travel in different directions, while the rays in a laser beam move in exactly the same direction. Since it doesn't spread out, it doesn't grow weak. It can travel long distances through space without spreading out and growing weaker. In the space age, it may become an important means of communication."

Jyotish asked - "What does laser stand for, ma'am?"

Ma'am replied - "The word laser is formed from the first letter of some long scientific words - "Light amplification stimulated emission of radiation."

What is a satellite?

Sanjeev asked - "Ma'am, what is a satellite?"

Ma'am replied - "A satellite is a body which revolves around a larger body. The earth is a satellite of the Sun since it revolves round the sun. The moon in a similar way is the satellite of the earth. These are nature's satellites.

But there are satellites which are made by human beings. These satellites are spacecrafts which circle the earth. Most of the countries have sent artificial satellites into space. They are of different sizes, from a tiny

package of instrument to a huge balloon more than 30 metres in diameter. They can be shaped like balls, hatboxes, tin cans, cigar boxes. They are used for scientific research. Some of them send back informations about weather. They relay television and radio broadcasts over long distances."

Sanjeev asked - "Ma'am, how far are they from the earth?"

Ma'am replied - "It depends on the task it must perform. Some of them are as near as 177 kilometres from the earth. Some are as far as 35,500 kilometres from the earth."

How does a satellite transmit TV programmes?

Megha asked - "Ma'am how does a satellite transmit TV programmes?"

Ma'am said - "To transmit TV programmes or to do any kind of work,

a satellite needs electrical power to operate its equipment. Do you know what is the main source of its power? The main source of this power is the sun. On their outside surface, satellite carry many solar cells. A solar cell is a device that uses sunlight to generate electricity. And this electricity keeps the satellite's batteries charged.

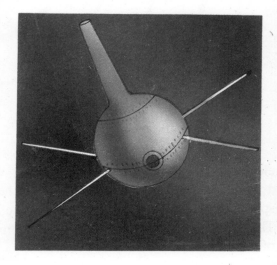

By means of communication satellites, radio and television signals are sent from one continent to another. The communication satellites have receivers and transmitters. It is with the help of receivers, the satellites pick up radio and television broadcasts from a ground station. The strength of these broadcast signals are then increased by the electronic devices. And then the transmitters send the broadcasts to a distant ground station, which may be on another Continent. With the help of a satellite we are able to see the programmes of different countries on T.V. Due to the satellites we could watch the Asiad, cricket match, the Wimbledon match and innumerable other programmes."

What are radio waves?

John asked - "Ma'am, what are radio waves?"

Ma'am replied - "You will be surprised to know that just now the space around us is filled with radio waves from nearby broadcasting stations. But we can hear them only when they become sound waves. And how do they become sound waves? Only when we turn on our radio.

A radio wave might be called a disturbance that moves out into the space. When electrons move back and forth rapidly, we have a radio wave. The radio waves have a much longer wavelengths than either heat or light waves. Radio waves travel through space in much the same way that waves travel when a pebble is dropped into water. The waves radiate in all directions from their source. Radio waves travel at a speed of about 180,000 miles a second!"

How do we know the height of a mountain?

Shabnam asked - "Ma'am, how do we know the height of a mountain? There are mountains which have never been climbed by people but still we know the height!"

Ma'am replied - "It is done by surveying, one of the oldest techniques on earth. It is concerned with determining the shape and size of any part of the earth's surface. Surveying is based on a method known as triangulation. In geometry, you will learn that if you know one side and two angles of any triangle or two sides and one angle, you can find out the rest of its measurements.

The instrument of measuring is called transit. When one has the area of one triangle, one keeps on dividing the land to be measured into triangles until one has the area of the entire piece of land. The transit works horizontally as well as vertically. This is called levelling because there is a spirit level at the base of the instrument that indicates when it is level. By raising the sight to any landmark on a mountain, the same process of measuring angles can be done and the length of one side (the height) can be measured."

How is the depth of an ocean measured ?

Linda asked - "Ma'am, how is the depth of an ocean measured?"

Ma'am replied - "In the old days, this was done by lowering a rope with a weight attached. But now the scientists have a much better idea because of the invention of a device called an echo sounder.

A device on the board the ship sends out a sound signal. The sound travels through the water at nearly one mile a second. It is echoed back to an instrument on the ship. The deeper the water, the longer it takes for the echo to reach the ship.

An echo sounder not only finds the depth of the sea but also the profile of the ocean floor. If the ship passes over an undersea mountain, the echo sounder records the exact shape of the mountain."